Mysterious MoonDance

Musings of an American Lycanthropologist

SALLY L. GAGE

DEDICATION

I, Sally L. Gage, being of quasi-sound mind and definitely not sound body, to hereby dedicate (and release into the wild) this book to the WerePup Mommies & Daddies across the globe, especially Asia and Anders Eriksen (because without them our extended pack family wouldn't exist), but also Angie Ramos, April Jeffers Pettit, Terry Oakes Paine, Candy Whitehead, Susan Gutierrez, Yvette Solomon, Lauren Madeline, Katie Schroeder-Muma, Renae Glenwalker Murphy, Mikey Aspinwall, Laila Wright, Julia DeBruyn, Lee Simms, and the other treasured members of the extended pack, which is growing daily!

I would also like to dedicate this to friends near and far throughout my life who had faith in the weirdo from Kemmer Road who danced in the moonlight.! Aroooooooo!

And lastly, without my coven of little dark souls—Marta Jones and Caitlin Grimes--I would have been lost, so this is for them most of all.

CONTENTS

ACKNOWLEDGMENTS

There are so many people I need to thank here--and believe me when I say that I owe them all so much! First of all, I would like to acknowledge that each of the papers published in this volume were completed for various courses taken at the University of South Florida, St. Petersburg and Tampa campuses from 2007 to 2012. I would like to thank the following professors for their mentorship, guidance, and for allowing me the space to express my continued interest in werewolves, cryptids, and the supernatural in an academic setting. These professors include: Dr. Frances Auld (for being another pea in the monster pod of academia) and Dr. Anna Dixon (who was tough and skeptical of everything…but I eventually won her over), as well as many other USF professors who allowed me to wander in odd directions with my writings.

I would also like to thank Richard and Geraldine Gage for helping to put me through college (the first time).

Additionally, I offer a laurel and hardy thanks to the Gaming Group for keeping me sane through college and for participating eagerly when I asked to interview them. To the PaleoNerds, thank you for the laughter and the tears throughout my extended college career.

Finally, it goes without saying that I need to thank my huni, Leisa Clark, for being there at my most intimate moments of self-doubt, for proof-reading every word in this tome, and for believing in me no matter how weird the subject.

FORWARD
BY LEISA A. CLARK

When Sally told me, around 2002, that she wanted to go back to college and "study werewolves, cryptids, and other fun things like that," my first instinct was to think, "well, okay, but..." As a hardcore academic myself, I was pretty well indoctrinated in the rhetoric of the Ivory Tower, which more or less stated that one could *not* study werewolves, cryptids, and other fun things like that and still be a *real* academic.

Sally enrolled in the University of South Florida, where she declared Anthropology as her major and where she spent the next five years or so proving to every professor she met that she could indeed make a serious study of things that she thought were important: werewolves, cryptids, and things that existed on the margins of humanity like vampires, witches, and zombies. As she moved forward through her schooling, she often butted heads with professors who could not understand how this focus was legitimate. They tried to force her into a narrow box that stated what was and was not "legitimate scholarship." But Sally resisted. She resisted hard. (I am still trying to picture the look on her Grant Writing professor's face when Sally turned in a well-researched, annotated, and well-documented mock grant proposal to study the Furry Community as a Subculture.)

For the most part, though, I have to give props to the many professors she encountered, first in Anthropology, and later, in Religious Studies, Humanities, Literature, and Women's Studies, as she was accepted into Graduate School. She stated very openly on her grad school application that she fully intended to study werewolves and write a thesis paper focusing on that research. Although she was accepted into two different graduate programs, I am not sure the program directors ever truly believed her. I am not sure her professors knew what to expect, either. Then the papers started rolling in.

One after the other, Sally met every assigned paper with a resounding "sounds like a werewolf/zombie/witch/vampire paper to me!" And indeed, that is exactly what she produced, time and again. She was lucky to have had many wonderfully supportive (if bewildered) mentors and instructors (several whom she calls "friend" now), because even if they were openly skeptical, they soon fell under the magical spell that is Sally's enthusiasm for cryptids and things that do not quite fit in our world. I believe she opened many eyes!

As time marched on, Sally held steadfastly true to her research and scholarship, even after leaving college. She has continued to not only keep up with all of the newest writings and reports, but to build a name for herself in the werewolf, dogmen, and cryptid communities. Recently, she coined the term "Lycanthropologist" to best describe her unique approach to researching werewolves and other cryptids through the lens of anthropology and cultural importance of such "marginalized monsters" that seem always to have been part of human existence.

Most of all, I have enjoyed watching Sally grow as a scholar, researcher, and werewolf badass. As I read these essays, I could see how she grew as a scholar from undergraduate through graduate studies, and I can also see how she got to where she is now: Lycanthropologist Extraordinaire. Now, as she has begun to attend conventions as a guest speaker, I am excited to see where her work will go next.

I hope you enjoy reading these essays as much as I did!

~Leisa A. Clark, St. Petersburg, FL August 2018

PREFACE:
THE LEARNED
LYCANTHROPOLOGIST

From the time I could wiggle in my diapers my family has always used storytelling to sooth, teach and empathize as well as negotiate the world around us. My father was particularly adept and would always regale the family with all sorts of tall tales as we sat around a fire watching the sparks carry us off into his imaginary worlds. He was a gifted orator and unbeknownst to me he passed down that most precious talent. It took some time, but once higher education took hold it tried reign in my natural predilection of colorizing my research papers for I had a goal in mind. Everything I learned I could and did apply to my deep-rooted passion for stories about werewolves. Anthropomorphized canids that lived in the cultural folklore of every human grouping on earth. Granted they have different names and perhaps origin stories but they all have the fact a large bipedal canid has been used throughout history.

My passion sparked one Sunday afternoon at my cousin's house. We were supposed play quietly, brush our teeth and hair then go to bed. Easy, right? LOL. So, the folks thought. The parental units went off to our grandparent's home to attend to business that didn't interest us and Lance (the oldest and guardian) promptly ran off with his girlfriend leaving Dawn, Shane and I to our own devices. So, we turned on the TV and low and behold the 1941 Classic *The Wolfman* starring Lon Chaney Jr. was on the local creature feature. It was like were stealing a car and going out drinking to our 8 and 9-year-old selves. We watched the whole thing…and didn't sleep for weeks. Seed planted.

Later when I was in high school, I was home alone so I did what any shy, nerdy high schooler did…I ordered a pizza and tuned in to the local creature feature. By this time, I started to really like horror movies, old-time psychological thrillers and ghost stories were my favorite but tonight it was the broadcast premiere of the 1981classic *The Howling.* I watched the whole thing…and didn't sleep for weeks. Seeds fertilized.

On April 1, 1987 local radio station WTCM radio released a song as an April fool's joke, much like a lyrical version of Orson Wells' *War of the Worlds.* Steve Cook's *The Legend* was about the Dogman of Michigan, a mythical werewolf type beast that appeared on the seventh year of every decade, it was 1987! I scrambled to get a copy of the song and when I did I listened repeatedly to the whole thing…and I didn't sleep for weeks. Seeds blossomed.

I decided to learn everything I could about the Dogman, werewolves, shapeshifters or anything I could possibly learn. First however, came the basics, myths and legends are born of reality so I started with reality of canine behavior when I got a job in a kennel working weekends, I also adopted and raised an Alaskan Timber wolf. Shuka was an education in the reality of wild animal care that's for sure. I went to school for animal science and then got distracted by the shiny world of Florida but soon I found my path again on the track of the North American Werewolf.

My undergraduate degree is in Anthropology where I studied the four subfields of anthropology which gave me the foundations for research in a thorough and scientific format that would only lend to my own skills regarding record keeping and accuracy when recording my own stories from people about dogmen. I began to focus on the intersectionality of the biological and the cultural: When Myths become Reality. See where I'm going?

Every paper I could, I tied my learning process to my beloved bipedal canids, much to many of my professor's chagrin. If I couldn't work the pups into a paper, another supernatural/mythical being would be slid into place. Vampires, zombies, witches, three legged gators…all myths and legends were there for me to analyze with my curriculum. So that's what I did. Represented here is that body of work from shiny undergrad newbie to surly master's curmudgeon and how the learned werewolf journey has progressed. Forgive the pretentious academic whomp whomp it was what I was supposed to do for a grade, but that pretentious knowledge has allowed be to branch into my own studies into the modern werewolf legend as it happens today and how these ancient stories have evolved and how their resurgence follows societies most desperate hours.

When I entered Graduate School, I was told that everything I did should be used to build your specialty field and every paper you write should be used towards your thesis. So, it is here I must state that I am a cannibal of my own work. As I moved through my academic career, I had little time (nor inclination) to build entire new works from scratch for subjects I may never use again each time I wrote a paper to appease each new professor soooooo I pulled sections and ideas from older papers to fill in newer works that seemed to fit my own lycanthropic research as a whole. So, don't be surprised if ideas, words and entire passages are repeated throughout this book. For the study of werewolves in grad school is just as rare as werewolves in real life.

SALLY L. GAGE

Lycanthropology

[lie-can-thr*uh*-**pol**-*uh*-jee]
noun

1. Lycan = wolf, anthro = man, pology = study of

2. the science that deals with the origins, physical and cultural dev
elopment, biological characteristics, and
social customs and beliefs of werewolves.

2. the study of werewolves
similarity to and divergence from other animals.

3. the science of werewolves.

4. Lycanthropologist: Person who studies wolfmen or werewolves

PART ONE
WACKY WEREWOLVES

MY ADVENTURES THROUGH ACADEMIA CHASING WEREWOLVES

The essays in part one are most of the papers I was able to salvage from both my undergrad and graduate studies programs that take the course subjects and apply it to werewolves, shapeshifters and dogmen. Some are better than others, but all were done with the specific courses teachings in mind. I first went to Michigan State University and got an AS degree in Animal Science. My papers from that time were PD (predigital) and sadly didn't survive the long journey to Florida nor the several homes, hurricanes or life in the sunshine state.

My next level of schooling was at the university of South Florida where I received a bachelor's degree in Anthropology. It was here the body of my works lie. My instructors were open to my questions and allowed me to apply anthropological theory to my passion of werewolves. Certain professors questioned my decision to pursue such a non-academic subject of which I responded the only reason that there is little written academically about this is perhaps the anthropologists weren't brave enough to face the academy and follow their passions of which there would probably be more Lycanthropologists. This gave pause for consideration. The door opened, and I walked proudly through.

Grad School however was another creature altogether. I made no mistake about where my passions and loyalties rested. A tough sell to a Women's and Gender Studies department who looked at me with such distain that they sabotaged my career. But I learned some valuable lessons, both in school and about the Academy. Once I could transfer from my department to the English Department. My writing became stronger and my faith in my own journey as a writer and researcher bean to really blossom. It was also at this time I coined the term "Lycanthropologist" (person who studies werewolves) as I already an anthropologist (person who studies people). Methodologies are the same except I look at the subject of the stories as well as the people.

1

"A COOL SUMMER MORNING IN EARLY JUNE, IS WHEN THE LEGEND BEGAN": THE EFFECTS OF STEVE COOK'S "THE LEGEND" ON COMMUNITIES IN 1980's MICHIGAN

Legend and folklore dictate that every living culture on this planet contains some form of the man-beast story. Throughout written history, from Africa to China to the Americas, tales of the skin-walker or shapeshifter were customarily seen as cautionary tales of unbridled sexual passion or shed light on our darker animal side to quench a blood thirst, and sightings of these creatures were attributed to fringe lunatics that committed ghastly atrocities claiming to be a werewolf. Folklore often describes animal/human hybrids as being trickster myths, anthropologists suggest that tricksters are responsible for bringing into the world many elements, often as a by-product of their shenanigans including change, hope and direction for the listener (Stein 24). Ironically, Steve Cook's "The Legend" debuted on the trickiest day of the year: the first of April in 1987. His trickster myth also had a profound effect on the listeners.

Unlike any other research paper, I am going to begin this with a story, a story that started with a song. For this author, in 1987 in Northern Michigan a single folksong captured the fears and unified a community at a time when economic and political ties were stained, and the residents felt abandoned and scared for the future. An artist named Steve Cook captured these fears in his song The Legend. This ballad sparked a frenzy of dogmen related sightings, tales of werewolves, and other paranormal happenings that gave birth to the supernatural subculture in Michigan after the song debuted.

Prior to the April 1987 unveiling of this particular song, the Dog Man existed only as whispered folklore until Traverse City radio deejay Steve Cook, penned a patter song called "The Legend." He first played his ballad on April Fool's Day on WTCM radio in Traverse City as a joke…and was not prepared for the reaction. The airing of the April Fool's lark caused many people to ask where the author had collected the tales because they had experienced similar events, most long before the events described in the lyrics of the song. The potential backlash of criticism had kept people from telling their stories until the song opened up a public forum in which people could share, commiserate and bond over events that they had in common. I was one of them.

I grew up in a Northern Michigan town mentioned in the now infamous song. The town was called Manistee, a sight for a reported cryptid encounter at a place called Clay-Bank Lake. I felt somehow akin to the folks who told their ghost stories from my home state; we bonded, I felt safe in the newfound knowledge that they had my back. We were in that dark time together. So, for the sake of this project, I put forth myself as both researcher and experiencer. Though I have never yet come face to face with the Dog Man, the idea of 'something' in the woods was social glue for the people of Northern Michigan at a time when paper mills, lumber yards and salt refineries were closing. Hard times had fallen upon the people of Northern Michigan of which I felt the effects first hand. Of course, this is a microanalysis of just local pressure unto this localized area, but the principals are the same when applied to large scale and nationwide models.

Past precedence of supernatural occurrences, and their popularity in relation to witch and werewolf trials of the past, will be used as evidence that these occurrences are nothing new, but are a trend that comes into and out of style according to political and religious powers and their influence over popular culture and the mind set of Americans that seem to be caught in the modern cycle of the werewolf. Michigan's rich folklore, has a beast of its own, a terrifying creature that roams its deep forests. But first, we will discuss the overarching social stresses in northern Michigan at the time of the release of this song.

The economic upheaval of the 1970s had important political consequences. When Ronald Reagan became president in 1980 he based his economic program on the theory of supply-side economics. George Bush commented that it was "Voodoo Economics" (a comment he later felt embarrassed by), which advocated reducing tax rates so people could keep more of what they earned (Jenkins 181). The theory was that lower tax rates would induce people to work harder and longer, and that this in turn would lead to more saving and investment, resulting in more production and stimulating overall economic growth. While this incentive inspired tax cuts to mostly benefit wealthier Americans, the economic theory behind the cuts argued that benefits would extend to lower-income people as well. This did not happen entirely as Reagan would have hope and overwhelming numbers of communities started to feel the pressure of long hours for the little jobs left in the rural farming and logging areas just like the ones I was growing up in Manistee. Although the three big factories, Morton Salt, PCA and Martin Marietta all still survive today many other paper, logging and other refineries closed up shop. Unemployment was high, and hope was low.

Social programs were also cut from the national budget. Reagan also undertook a campaign throughout his tenure to reduce or eliminate government regulations affecting the consumer, the workplace, and the environment, all the things that Northern Michigan residents are and need at this time of no jobs and uncomfortable change. In addition, Reagan feared that the United States had neglected its military and began a ramped up cold war propaganda campaign to increase defense spending, subsequently increasing the nations fears of soviet incursion.

Reaganomics was the combination of tax cuts and higher military spending overwhelmed more modest reductions in spending on domestic programs that resulted in the federal budget deficit swelling beyond the levels it had reached during the recession of the early 1980s. From $74,000 million in 1980, the federal budget deficit rose to $221,000 million in 1986. It fell back to $150,000 million in 1987, but then started growing again. The Trickle-down effect did not trickle so well (Jenkins 181).

In the case of Michigan, the state's unemployment is rising fast as more and more steel, automotive and lumber plants close and casino's crop up. Large industrial jobs were being lost and although many reports state a job increase, many of the jobs were geared for a non-industrial work set and many of the people who were previously employed had to either switch vocations or move from the state entirely, which many did. Many Michigan workers and their families left the state in search of opportunities in other regions. Households decide to migrate based on more than local conditions. Workers who were wealthy enough to move did, other stayed because of the heavy expense or because of family that refused to go. My family fell into the latter. After my father was laid off, I refused to leave the area where my mother was buried, and my life was. I was getting ready to start college and I did not want to lose what was left of the tar-paper-shit-shack I called home. Fear of the perceived threat from foreign instigators scared us into inaction, spinning internally for lack of safety. Friends, family, neighbors and towns were being drastically changed and it was then a portion of the population began to find a home with unlikely bedfellows that all tie to the song The Legend.

Groups of dogmen hunters and paranormal enthusiasts began springing up all over the Northern Michigan territory. Ghost Hunting was something yet to be truly embraced by the mass culture and the internet was yet to be born so the groups were local in origin and generally consisted of a few like-minded individuals that gathered together and talk about the experiences they each had encountered with the supernatural. The group I was associated with consisted of three – four high school students and former high school students, a fairly wealthy local business owner who had connections with other business owners and landowners that allowed investigations, a schoolteacher and an ironworker. Two of the group, were designated by their heritage, as the "token" Indians and the rest were all white. According to the census, the population of Manistee Township consisted of 94% white, 1.2 % Native American and 5% other so the numbers are not that unusual. The group met up usually weekly in the beginning of June of 1987 and slowly tapered off until the Luther incident occurred at the end of July. The story sent the group into a full-fledged hunt mode with weekend shinning expeditions into the Manistee National Forest. Armed with flashlights, cameras and a little liquid courage we loaded up truck and went searching. After that summer, the group never actually saw a dogman and we never found any evidence of its existence, but we found something even more important. We found a group of people who came from different socio-economic backgrounds, different races and genders had come together and pooled resources with each in a common goal. Who we were didn't matter prior to the songs release, and we all may have gone our separate ways since then, but for the summer of 1987 we were tighter than family, we had firm trust and loyalty and passion for each other. A song written as a joke brought us together.

In Philip Jenkin's book Decade of Nightmares, suggests that crime and criminals became more violent and more sadistic leaning towards the term "monster" (Jenkins 140). Media had become more global and the threat towards Americans and American children were driven home with images of abducted children that had been tortured and murdered (refereeing to the Adam Walsh case) and the exposure of the term abuse for both women and children became a media staple. Media efforts to protect the children and family became paramount in a wide spread campaign that saw a and attention turn towards multiple murders, heinous acts, unspeakable cruelty (Jenkins 147) and fear of our neighbors geared the populace towards a more solitary lifestyle. With the new fear mongering upon us we also saw that our government was indeed fallible and corrupt with crimes of the powerful (Jenkins 49) taking a more visual in both pop culture and real life, the safety that we as Americans felt with our father (president) being completely trustworthy was being shaken and proven false. Church scandals began to shake the foundations of the church and lending discordance within the other overseeing father (religion). With both overseeing safety nets of our community being called into question, its little doubt we, as a collective psyche, would search for another answer subconsciously. This particular time in Northern Michigan is was on more of a micro level but it still follows suit with the macro model.

The 1970s were also a time when fictionalized horror novels shifted to show former "monster" as a misunderstood victim, if not a hero. Anne Rice's groundbreaking *Interview with the Vampire* was published in 1976, focusing on the human within the monster. It was only a matter of time before the formerly lambasted werewolf was reexamined in a similar way. It is in the novel, *Wolfen*, a 1978 horror story by Whitley Strieber, where we find the center of the book shown through the plight of the intelligent city dwelling wolves and their survival. Subsequent films, such as *The Howling* and *American Werewolf in London* (both in 1981),

In the Company of Wolves (1984), *Silver Bullet, Teen Wolf,* and *The Howling II* (all in 1985) illustrated that American audiences were clearly ready to reexamine werewolves in multiple media, including movies and television as well as radio with only a moderate facelift into a dogman.

"The Legend" debuted on April 1, 1987 on WTCM radio in Traverse City Michigan. Written by Steve Cook and performed by Steve Cook's alter ego Bob Farley, the ballad is a patter-style song that has a musical underscore to support the lyrics. The patter song is a staple of comic opera, but it has also been used in musicals and other situations such as this. It is characterized by a moderately fast to very fast tempo with a rapid succession of rhythmic patterns in which each syllable of text and the musical accompaniment is lightly orchestrated and fairly simple, to emphasize the text (Virginia Tech). The drums are used in a traditional native American drum beat style to emulate the beat of a human heart. This type of rhythmic beat is subconsciously soothing and subliminally brings our psyche in tune with the story being told. The cords played (in the original release) are in a discordance that sets us at unease. So just my listening to the music alone the listener is both comfortable and at unease. Just as if we were listening to a ghost story told around a campfire in the middle of the night (Cook).

This basic storytelling type song was wildly popular in Michigan in the area where The Legend was founded. Gordon Lightfoot's "The Wreck of the Edmund Fitzgerald," Johnny Cash's "A Boy Named Sue" and Billy Joel's "We didn't start the Fire" were classic examples of story-embedded songs that were played ad nauseum on all the radio stations in the Northern Michigan area as they span the genres of music that were locally present at that time.

An avid folklore collector since his youth, Steve Cook was especially fascinated by hauntings and unusual animals. Choosing characteristics of Bigfoot, the Boggy Creek monster from Arkansas, the Jersey Devil, and several other "cryptids," Cook created a mythical half-man, half-dog, and wrote several verses about appearances of the creature. He placed the events in Northern Michigan towns, and gave the Dogman a mysterious chronological nature. Each sighting occurs in the seventh year of the decade. When describing why he implemented the 'seventh year' rotation, Cook noted, "I was paying homage to an old movie called *The Night Stalker.* In that film, a reporter (Darren McGavin) was pursuing a killer who terrorized Seattle every ten years. That idea played very well in the Dogman story. Everything in nature is cyclical:

bird migrations, the seasons, locusts, etc. I picked the seventh year simply because it happened to be 1987" (Cook)

As the poem took shape, Cook began sampling different ways of recording it for broadcast. The most promising featured a simple drum rhythm extracted from a cheap analog Casio keyboard. The meter of the poem fit perfectly into 4/4 time (Cook). Using some of the other voices on the keyboard, Cook developed a melody and chord structure that sounds vaguely Native American.

According to Cook, all but one of the verses in the original song were based on actual events, however, some locations were adjusted to fall within the listening area of the radio station for which the song was prepared (WTCM in Traverse City, Michigan). A few of the dates are accurate, but some were moved to a year ending in "7", to fit with the seventh-year cycle theme that he built into the structure of the story. The only verse that is entirely fictional is the 1907 crazy old widow story.

That said, the only events that occurred exactly as stated in the song were the 1967 hippies in a van story, and the 1987 Luther cabin attack (both are detailed in the Encounters section of Steve Cook's website). The Bellaire verse was based on a rash of sighting reports (strange animals and UFOs) that occurred in Antrim County in the 60s and 70s. We actually cut that verse from the 2007 version of the song to make room for the new final verse.

So, I have told you about the eighties, national economies, the song and strange people who search for fiction werewolves in the darkness of the Northern Michigan nights, but how does this tie together? Well here it is: I am going to tell you about what this song actually means to a participant observer, what made this the catalyst to a career that is still being pursued and how folklore and storytelling started it all.

For me, I was young, seventeen, preparing for college and lonely. I lived in a rural community that was slowly being eaten away by poverty, despair and looking at my approaching adult life with little prospects. Hunting, fishing and wilderness refuge was the only escape from the physical evidence of the dilapidated homes and boarded up businesses that depressed my world. April first focused our attention on a story that placed the area on edge. I theorize that everyone has a ghost story or paranormal experience. Whether they believe in ghosts, werewolves and aliens or not, we all have a story we like to tell. The Legend, gave us all one in common that we could all look for in our backyards, or relate an experience that had occurred in the forest. We were given a venue for which we could focus our fears and social anxieties. The phenomenon happens when large overarching social stresses are completely out of the control of the populace. As with witch-hunt and werewolf trials of the past, the supernatural seems to be a failsafe mechanism for the communal psyche. I believe this is exactly what happened in a depressed Michigan in 1987. Mass unemployment, factory closings and mass migration of peoples left the remaining residents in an uncontrollable situation in which they could not foresee a solution for their problematic world. I not saying we all went bug nuts and started chasing angels, but I believe as a collected psyche we turned to the only power we know that was left to call upon for unconscious assistance, the unknown. Call it God or called it the creator or whatever deity you may believe, we seek solace in an unknown being or state for safety and comfort in a time of need.

The Legend, although a non-entity, spoke of an earth-bound unknown being that crept around in the north woods darkness, the very area we were living in. The song brought to earth a being that could be sought after/fear/loved …touched. The lyrics used a local accent and rustic word use that akin us to the artist and tale being told. The use of local towns and townships and known landmarks further brought home the intimacy of the story to the listeners and closer to the unknown because it was among us.

According to anthropologists, there are five kinds of human reality: Tone is called the Universe with a capital U and is defined as object reality or all that exists. Second is the Species world where every species has their own perspective of the Universe, like a dog sees and hears differently than humans do. Third is the Perceptual world where each individual has their own unique perception of reality just like the fourth, which is the Personal world in which it is our own personal understanding of our culture and finally our Cultural World, a world in which our culture teaches each other and how we transmit that information (Baker 37). I believe that this song has spoken to each one of these perspectives in life.

Although, personally, the song scared me into many sleepless nights and fueled a growing need to exploring folklore, especially about animal/man hybrids…werewolves. My fear birthed a passion for understanding, why people gravitate towards mythical canines. It quite literally changed my life. I can say that I am no longer afraid to be intimidated by mass pressure to conform or agree with points of view I do not agree with. I find strength in the fact my research into this strange world is not a fool's errand, but a passion bestowed upon me by a quirky little folk song that was meant to be a farce, but created something bigger, more important and ultimately more fulfilling…a family. Because even though today scholars look at me sideways, and the grad school personal shakes their collective heads at me, it is always in the quiet times those people come to me and tell me their story…their ghost story or dogman story or some other paranormal event they had experienced and it binds us together…even if it may be for a short time.

Why the Wolf? Well, from the time that humans stood upright, we have been in a battle of survival, as both predator and prey. We have had to out think our competitors for food, resources, and living space. One of those fiercest competitors has always been the wolf. A creature that to the mindset of the people of Medieval Europe was an animal that thought with the cunningness of humans and the fierceness of demons. The wolf held no reservation about killing humans and their stock as a source of food. Fear of these animals colored local folklore throughout Europe, painted the wolf as a beast spat up from Hell itself, and was capable of anything. Stories of werewolves as mindless human/animal murderers served as both a structured social warning and community solidifier for generations. Stories of the big, bad wolf comfortably placed people together with each other against the "wilds" of our animalist nature, the environment and its inhabitants. We were safe against the "others", us against them. The image of the wolf remained this way almost until their near extinction in North America. When the wolf became one of us, a fragile needing help, the illusion of the beast began to melt. After the North American Timber Wolf was placed on the endangered species list, multiple and serious studies into their behavior and lives were conducted revealing a truly different animal.

Since the 1970's the revamping of the lupine image had taken on a more spiritual tone, an Earth wizened creature with characteristics that Americans as a whole, value. Strong leadership with a rigidly structured hierarchy, monogamous relationships that last a life time, communal and familial bonds that are near supernatural in its strengths were revealed to a public that felt that those very aspects were slipping away from them in a world of concrete and commerce. With these new images, is it any wonder why in a society seeking these very things, we would see them…albeit in a form we would least expect…a wolf/human hybrid. I for one would expect to that very thing, aspect of the mystical wolf graphed onto our familiar bipedal shape.

As for the dog, well it is the domestication of the wolf. A mysterious and spiritual being tamed and brought into our homes, the dog is man's best friend. Three simple words to describe the most familiar of mankind's' animal companions that still harbor the wildness of the forest but is a devoted ally (Varner 149). The anthropomorphizing of the dog is done in nearly every household, but to actually bring characteristics of both man and dog together in one being would be the next logical step in this evolution of thought. What better way to be closest to your best friend than to become one. (White 22) In a non-sexual context, bestiality is another paper entirely.

Which brings us to the encounters with the dogmen themselves, though at the time frightening for the experiencer, rarely have the reports been one of "It came through the trailer walls fixen ta eat me" but one of benign observation of a shadowy creature crossing the road or a furry beast drinking water at the river side going about its business as we, the intruder, interrupts that very routine. We have become the outsider seeing into their lives. Through the eyes of this writer, it would appear that as the wolf changed shape from nefarious to noble as to do our reasons for seeking them

The Legend was a simple poem put to music and played for a hungering audience that craved a resolution to the overbearing world around them. The state of the economy, uncertain futures and the decline of nearly everything we knew as a culture in Northern Michigan left the populace in a state that felt like being punch-drunk and depressed. The people responded to The Legend as if to not only seek validation for their personal stories but also to seek validation for their existence. People from across the age, race, gender and socio-economic backgrounds were drawn together in a collective group that overlooked their differences and pooled their resources for the greater good. The groups found families that had been fractured and a goal they could work towards.

Privately we all knew that there was no werewolf in our communities, but the idea of the unknown created a solid, unified community. That was what we needed, to feel safe once again in our homes and feel a part of something bigger than the depression around us. The story allowed us to feel the anxiety around us and place a face on the culprit...The Dogman. No other papers have been written nor observation made about this particular time in Michigan dealing with the Dogmen, but I hope this can be a start to a social awareness and social need to have fun with folklore and the actual importance it plays in our community.

Correlations between the anxiety of living in our postmodern world with the electronic buzz and political unrest and supernatural sightings have been shown through brief examples like the story of The Legend to have an effect, for although the dogmen may not be real they are real in their consequences. (Crawley) That is why we are bound to be forever caught in the cycle of the werewolf.

Works Cited

Baker, John R. & Michael Winkelman. Supernatural as Natural: A Biological Approach to Religion. Upper Saddle River: Pearson Prentice Hall. 2010.

Baring-Gould, Sabine. The Book of Werewolves. New York: Dover, 1865-2006.

Barry, Jonathan, Marianne Hester & Gareth Roberts. Witchcraft in Early Modern Europe. Cambridge: Cambridge University Press, 1996.

Coleman, Loren and Jerome Clark. Cryptozoology A-Z: The Encyclopedia of Loch Monsters, Sasquatch, Chupacabras and other Authentic Mysteries of Nature. New York: Fireside, 1999.

Coleman, Loren. Mysterious America. New York: Pocket Books, 2007.

Cook, Steve. The Legend. Traverse City: Mindstage Productions, 1987-2007.

---. The Legend of Michigan's Dogmen: http://www.michigan-Dogman.com/

James, Wendy. The Ceremonial Animal. Oxford: Oxford University Press, 2003-2005.

Steiger, Brad. The Werewolf Book. Canton: Visible Ink, 1999.

Stein, Rebecca & Philip Stein. The Anthropology of Religion, Magic and Witchcraft. Boston: Pearson Education, 2005.

Suckling, Neil. Werewolves. London: Steerling Publishing Inc., 2006.

Summers, Montegue. The Werewolf in Lore and Legend. Minola: Dover, 2003-1933.

Varner, Gary R. Creatures in the Mist: Little People and Spirit Beings Around the   World: A Study in Comparative Mythology. New York: Algora Publishing,   2007.

White, David Gordon. Myths of the Dogman. Chicago: University of Chicago Press, 1991.

2

CYCLE OF THE WEREWOLF: CORRELATIONS BETWEEN CRYPTID SIGHTINGS AND SOCIAL ANXIETY

Legend and folklore dictate that in every living culture on this planet contain some form of the man-beast story. From Africa to China to the Americas, tales of the skinwalker or shapeshifter were customarily seen as cautionary tales of unbridled sexual passion or shed light on our darker animal side to quench a blood thirst, and sightings of these creatures were attributed to fringe lunatics that committed ghastly atrocities claiming to be a werewolf. What I am going to be looking at in this paper is not the folklore of a people, a psychology of fringe madmen or even the wild stories of attention seeking loners, but what I am analyzing are the reports of relatively normal people, doing everyday normal things when they experience an unusual circumstance; they encounter what they cannot understand other than a beast that walks upright and it looks like a dog and how these reports correlate with overarching social stress of the time.

Past precedence of these occurrences relates to witch and werewolf trials of the enlightenment, which will be used as evidence that these occurrences are nothing new, but a trend that comes into and out of style according to political and religious powers and their influence over popular culture and the popular mind set of Americans caught in the modern Cycle of the werewolf.

Before I get into the bulk of the evidentiary support of my paper it is important that I first eliminate what the terms in this paper are not. It is understood that the clinical psychiatric disorder known as "lycanthropy" is a syndrome in which an individual believes and exhibits the telling characteristics of being a werewolf or Lycanthrope. I am not saying that these individuals physically shift appearance from man into wolf, but they psychologically shift from man into beast. These individuals are enthralled and excited when the moon is full have a taste for raw meat as well as an aversion to silver and crucifixes. This is a psychological disorder that does not factor in this paper as the individuals are the ones "witnessing" and not partaking.

This brings to point the attention seekers in our society. Many people find no greater thrill than to waste researchers' time and resources looking for the boogey-man just to get a few minutes of fame and glory from local media or to have their cutting edge special effects program show the "realism" of documented footage or still photos. This research is on people who are not looking to be famous, quite the opposite in most cases, but who are hardworking and well-respected members of their communities. Some leave the experience with a sense of curiosity of the event; some leave the experience knowing what terror really is: but all leave changed. This also leads to accusations of mass hysteria or mass panic of people in our society. If that were the case, there would be record high sales of silver bullets, wolfsbane wreaths and monster hunters would be the "new sexy" profession that would be costing the tax payers untold millions of dollars for their safety. So far this is not the case.

I am not out to prove werewolves exist or that bigfoot is real, but simply look at the tales and how these stories are affected by our socio-political climate.

We are always told we are doomed to repeat the past, analysis of past events alongside our current world affairs illustrate that this is, for the most part true. We as people squabble over parcels of land and religious freedoms and make others submit or perish according to the powers that be. So, these truths are also evident when looking at recorded events of the supernatural.

It is often believed that during the enlightenment of Europe, pressure from the church sent untold hundreds if not thousands of men, women and children to their deaths because of accusations of witch craft. Alas this simply is not the case, according to records from court proceedings of that time; it was a result from a trend known as "pressure from beneath." (Sharpe 33). It was largely, but not always, a case in which members of the community were at odds for whatever reason. In many of the witch trials you will find that the church was a calming force that ebbed a tide of panic that could have easily swept through a township. When a witch or werewolf was singled out in the community, a strange phenomenon occurred: social unification as a whole. Solidarity lent comfort to the township and kinship where there may have been strife, well maybe not for the accused, but rather for the community at large. You see, at this time period the population was in constant turmoil. Crusades, territorial warfare, starvation and plague lent the collective psyche of the people scared, fractured and fatalistic. The fragmenting of the church into Catholic and Protestant also left people confused and uncertain. As governments stabilized and the witch reformations of 1663 came into play, the overall view of these cases were consuming to much of the state's money and intellectual time and cases were being dismissed. The reported sightings and subsequent trials for the witches began to decrease (Sharpe 73). The trial of Jean Louis Grainier, a fourteen-year-old boy accused of killing numerous babies and attacking a young girl was one of the most famous werewolf cases brought before the courts (Summers).

The case still is the source of many tales and pop culture tributes, but few have look into the sightings of Beast of Gévaudan. The Beast of Gévaudan (French: La bête du Gévaudan) was a mysterious wolf-like creature that terrorized the former province of Gévaudan (modern day *Lozère département*), in the Margeride Mountains in south-central France from about 1764 to 1767. (Summers) (Barry)Many attacks took place—between 60 and 100 people were killed—and debate continues as to the Beast's identity. The wealth of the Provence was high, and the beast successfully caused shepherds to not tend their flocks of sheep and cattle as well as harvesting was brought to a halt eventually leaving the Provence in financial destitution.

However just prior to the brutal "werewolf" slayings, King Henri IV had also to deal with the fanatic Protestant warlord Matthieu Merle, who had seized several cities, including Mende in 1579, and finally appointed him Governor of Mende. Following the suppression of the Tolerance Edict by Louis XIV (1685) and the repression organized against the

Protestants, the guerilla of the Camisards took place in the Cévennes from 1702 to 1704. The repression stopped only in 1787 when Louis XVI reestablished religious tolerance (cf. Barry; Clark).

Intense political and religious conflict within a nation became a single unit when close to one hundred people were killed by a Loup Garou, a single purpose was called for unifying the people of this Provence, La bête du Gévaudan.

Modern accounts of cryptid animals are met with less religious implications and more skepticism but reports still happen today. Stories of strange black panthers that stalked the woods of North America were met with snickers of ridicule and rolling eyes…until researchers caught one in the Everglades National Park in 2007. The Bray Road Beast is another such creature that has been sighted by numerous witnesses in Elkhorn, Wisconsin from 1936 to the present. A creature that, was thought to be a big dog or some kind of weird mix of dog and bear, until it stood upright on its hind legs. This creature has been seen by numerous individuals including police officers and county workers. When this story hit national news, further witnesses came forward to report their own encounter, but were afraid to before because of ridicule (Godfrey, *The Beast of Brey Road*). Linda Godfrey has made it her life goal to document these sightings and to weed out the "fraudulent" cases and chart actual "unknown animal" sightings. Based on the sightings she recorded, a timeline of the Beast of Bray Road occurrences has emerged (Godfrey, *Hunting the American Werewolf*).

A spike in the sightings occurred in the late sixties and early seventies where correlation between the stress of the Vietnam War, Watergate, Civil rights movement and second wave feminism was shaking the secured foundation of the pristine American Ideal to its core. The onset of the eighties and nineties, the sightings drifted down to a smaller number, but then have spiked again in 2000. The accounts of reported sightings have risen to a new dramatic height between 2002 and 2004 not just in Wisconsin alone, but in surrounding states as well, Michigan being one of them. Michigan has a beast of its own; a terrifying creature that roams its deep forests. Like the Beast of Bray Road, the Dog Man, as it has come to be known, has been seen in the state's northernmost forests and communities.

The Dog Man existed only as whispered folklore until 1987 when Traverse City radio deejay Steve Cook, wrote a song he called "The Legend." He first played his ballad on April fool's Day, 1987, on WTCM radio in Traverse City as a lark—and was not prepared for the reaction. Just as with the Beast of Bray Road, the airing of the April Fool's joke caused many people to ask where the author had collected the tales because they had experienced similar events, most long prior to the events in the lyrics of the song. The potential backlash of criticism also kept people from telling their stories until the song opened a public forum in which people could share, commiserate and bond over events that they had in common. I was one of them. I grew up in a Northern Michigan town mentioned in the now infamous song, called Manistee, a sight for a reported encountered at a place called Clay-bank Creek. I felt somehow akinned to the folks who told tales from my home state, we bonded, I felt safe in the new-found knowledge that they had my back; we were in this dark time together. So, for the sake of this project I put forth myself as both researcher and experiencer. Though I had never come face to face with the Dog Man, the idea of 'something' in the woods was social glue for the people of Northern Michigan at a time when paper mills, lumber yards and salt refineries were closing. Hard times had fallen upon the people of Northern Michigan of which I felt the effects first hand. Of course, this is a micro analysis of just local pressure unto this localized area, but the principals are the same when applied to large scale and nationwide models.

Starting in 1987 reports of the Dog Man drizzled down until around 2002-2003 when reports started to rise again. By 2007 the popular demand for the song's return had led to a new updated version recorded to include the lyrics "what happens when the truth out runs the fiction," acknowledging the fact the song was little more than a fancy but had turned into something more. So, the trend continues.

So, what is the connection between Wisconsin and Michigan and this age of technology that we are so rely on? Like our past we to are living through an age where our political leaders and clerical orders are casting doubt in our minds. Currently we are involved in a war, not over terrorism, but of money and power. Media scandals involving the church and all its orders are flooding our papers, television and internet news sources. It seems that shootings and mass murders are so common place and are becoming little more than a nuisance as we click by the stories to get to our favorite TV shows. People, although not directly involved with these traumatic events are none the less affected by them. Post-traumatic Stress Disorder affected millions of Americans after the events of 9/11. This problem was seen by the New York City Board of Education commissioned Applied Research and Consulting to treat New York City children for this disorder following the attacks. The results of the study show that 26.5% of the children displayed some disorder that affected their daily routines. This number was consistent with following research from other states stating the number of affected grew, as did the number of reported Dog Men or Beast sightings between the years of 2002 and 2005.

In the case of Michigan, the state's unemployment is rising fast as more and more steel, automotive and lumber plants close and casino's crop up. The state economy is at an all-time low, according to CNN news and my father, current resident. People are being left in another desperate time and it would seem the Dog Men have made a return. As for Wisconsin I do not know of their states economic fortune, but sightings peaked in 2004 and have slowly dropped off. Maybe their luck is shifting for the better.

From the time that humans stood upright we have been in a battle of survival, as both predator and prey. We have had to out think our competitors for food, resources, and living space. One of those fiercest competitors has always been the wolf. A creature that to the mindset of the people of Medieval Europe was an animal that thought with the cunningness of humans and the fierceness of demons. The wolf held no reservation about killing humans and their stock as a source of food. Fear of these animals colored local folklore throughout Europe and painted the wolf as a beast spat up from Hell itself and was capable of anything. Stories of werewolves as mindless human/animal murderers served as both a structured social warning and community solidifier for generations. Stories of the big, bad wolf comfortably placed people together with each other against the "wilds" of our animalist nature, the environment and its inhabitants. We were safe against the "others", us against them. The image of the wolf remained this way almost until their near extinction in North America. When the wolf became one of us, a fragile being needing help, the illusion of the beast began to melt. After the North American Timber Wolf was placed on the endangered species list, multiple and serious studies into their behavior and lives were conducted revealing a truly different animal.

Since the 1970's the revamping of the lupine image had taken on a more spiritual tone, an Earth wizened creature with characteristics that Americans as a whole, value. Strong leadership with a rigidly structured hierarchy, monogamous relationships that last a life time, communal and familial bonds that are near supernatural in its strengths were revealed to a public that felt that those very aspects were slipping away from them in a world of concrete and commerce. With these new images, is it any wonder why in a society seeking these very things, we would see them…albeit in a form we would least expect…a wolf/human hybrid. I for one would expect to that very thing, aspect of the mystical wolf graphed onto our familiar bipedal shape.

Which brings us to the encounters themselves, though at the time frightening for the experiencer, rarely have the reports been one of "It came through the trailer walls fixen ta eat me" but one of benign observation of a shadowy creature crossing the road or a furry beast drinking water at the river side going about its business as we, the intruder, interrupts that very routine. We have become the outsider seeing into their lives. Through the eyes of this writer it would appear that as the wolf changed shape from nefarious to noble as to do our reasons for seeking them.

Though pop culture has an influence on the type of sightings reported, it has little affected what the people have actually reported seeing, a large dog-like beast that walks upright. Seen at a time when our sleepy nation was startled into a reality of a terrorist attack on our soil and when our nation's political and church leaders are questionable at best, it can be suggested that these beasts are being seen to unite us in a shaky and uncertain future we all face. I realize that this research is merely an overview of a much larger thesis project that is too large to place into an eight to ten-page presentation paper; however, this work is the beginning of the research I intend to pursue into grad school. Actual stories have been eliminated to both protect the identities and to streamline the information.

Correlations between the anxiety of living in our postmodern world with the electronic buzz and political unrest, these supernatural sightings of bipedal canids have been shown through brief examples that we are bound to be forever caught in the cycle of the werewolf.

Works Cited

Baring-Gould, Sabine. The Book of Werewolves. New York: Dover, 1865-2006.

Coleman, Loren and Jerome Clark. Cryptozoology A-Z: The Encyclopedia of Loch Monsters, Sasquatch, Chupacabras and other Authentic Mysteries of Nature. New York: Fireside, 1999.

Coleman, Loren. Mysterious America. New York: Pocket Books, 2007.

Godfrey, Linda S. Hunting the American Werewolf. Madison: Trail Books, 2006.

---. The Beast of Brey Road. Madison: Prairie Oak Press, 2003.

Guiley, Rosemary Ellen. Encyclopedia of Vampires, Werewolves and other Monsters. New York: Checkmark Books, 2005.

Hamel, Frank. Werewolves, Bird-Women, Tiger-men and other human animals. New York: Dover Publishing, 1915-2007.

James, Wendy. The Ceremonial Animal. Oxford: Oxford University Press, 2003- 2005.

Barry, Jonathan, Marianne Hester and Gareth Roberts. Witchcraft in Early Modern Europe. Cambridge: Cambridge University Press, 1996.

Lecouteux, Claude. Witches, Werewolves and Fairies: Shapeshifters and Astral doubles in the Middle Ages. Rochester: Inner Traditions, 2003.

Maxwell-Stuart, P.G. Witchcraft in Europe and the New World, 1400-1800. New York: Palgrave, 2001.

Sharpe, James. Witchcraft in Early Modern England. London: Pearson Education, 2001.

Steiger, Brad. The Werewolf Book. Canton: Visible Ink, 1999.

Stein, Rebecca & Philip Stein. The Anthropology of Religion, Magic and Witchcraft. Boston: Pearson Education, 2005.

Suckling, Neil. Werewolves. London: Steerling Publishing Inc., 2006.

Summers, Montegue. The Werewolf in Lore and Legend. Minola: Dover, 2003-1933.

3

ŠUŊGMÁNITU THAŊKA OB'WAČHI: OF WOLVES, WOMEN, WOLF LAKE, AND GENDER STEREOTYPES

She who runs with wolves: the words conjure images of a wild woman running scantily clad through the forest with a large canid loping beside her, wild and free. Perhaps that's what I feel like at times, nearly naked and my companions are animals, free from the social obligations that I adhere to just for the sake of being accepted, conformist...ignored. Since this assignment was to write about anything that I wanted, and apply feminist theory, I decided to do just that in the form of an autoethnographic research paper. But first you have to know something about me; I am a Native American who passes as white, a bisexual woman who passes as straight or bisexual woman who passes as gay depending on your perspective. I am a transitional person, multifaceted to the point of near obsession with one thing, the fictional (or not so fictional) beings of werewolves. This human/nonhuman is the personification of the physical and emotional thing I live with every day. White/not white, straight/not straight, the duality is a key ingredient to Sally. Like it or not, I study werewolves, shapeshifters, skinwalkers and their surrounding folklore. I will be applying feminist theory to FICTIONAL characters portrayed by actors who are not werewolves. This paper will examine two aspects; one is the pivotal point in which the wolf turned from marginalized villain to that of central protagonist in historical narratives and the other is an analysis of the adoption of wolf imagery by eco-feminists and women's communities. Then with this adoption practice in mind, I will move on to the interpretations of werewolf imagery in television as a reflection of feminist theory superimposed upon film in dramatized reality.

Television and films allow us to journey to idealized worlds, a trained eye can read into them meanings never intended by the filmmaker, just as real-life scenarios are interpreted by legions of theorists looking for meaning in words from print or the sounds of disembodied voices across the airwaves, hope hidden behind lyrics of songs and other devices, just as academics seek meaning in the words of their peers. Whether to argue against a statement or idea to find validations for their own feelings, theory of week or personal crusade or to add a missing piece of substance, writers often seek to better themselves or the world around them though their own interpretive means.

I am choosing to analyze the television series *Wolf Lake* with an eye towards comparing and contrasting the gendered behavior in both human and wolf form. I will also examine the change from solitary (or lone) werewolves to pack werewolves in Wolf Lake. I argue that the characters portrayed on the television program act in a hyper-heteronormative fashion when in "human" form, but when they transform into their "beast" form, they shed the idea of gender performativity and slip into a "queer" existence by being completely gender free, even to the point of lacking the defined gender characteristics associated with the western ideals of masculine and feminine.

In Simone de Beauvoir's "Introduction" to *The Second Sex*, the author attempts to analyze the very meaning of what it is to be "woman" through biology, psychoanalysis and historical materialisms and how "feminine" has been fashioned from man in an attempt to "other" women so the hierarchy of our society is firmly engrained. What is it to be woman?

According to de Beauvoir, "Males and females are two types of individuals which are differentiated within a species for the function of reproduction; they can be defined only correlatively. But first it must be noted that even the division of a species into two sexes is not always clear-cut" (12). De Beauvoir then states that first she must begin by stating "I am a woman" and by that preliminary answer is significant as all further discussion will directly relate to that statement (de Beauvoir 12). A man does not say this. This alone say that all proper discussion or viewpoints that are normal and expected are male based and women are secondary, an exception to "the rules" of common communication. Woman is in a separate category and thus "othered", an outsider in which translation is necessary to continue. This othering is the viewpoint in which I will analyze the following cinematic representations of gendered performance as I see them in the various films and televisions series I previously mentioned.

Feminists have taken many different approaches to the analysis of cinema. These include discussions of the function of women characters in particular film narratives or in particular genres, such as film noir, where a woman character can often be seen to embody a subversive sexuality that is dangerous to men and is ultimately punished with death. In considering the way that films are put together, many feminist film critics, such as Laura Mulvey, have pointed to the "male gaze" that predominates in classical Hollywood film making (67). Through the use of various film techniques, such as a reverse shot, the viewer is led to align herself with the point of view of a male protagonist. Notably, women function as objects of this gaze far more often than as proxies for the spectator (Mulvey 68). With this film theory I can also apply psychoanalytic theory.

Psychoanalytic feminism is based on Freud and his psychoanalytic theories. It maintains that gender is not biological but is based on the psycho-sexual development of the individual. Psychoanalytical feminists believe that gender inequality comes from early childhood experiences, which lead men to believe that they themselves to be masculine, and women to believe themselves feminine. It is further maintained that gender leads to a social system that is dominated by males, which in turn influences the individual psycho-sexual development.

Early discourse of queer theory involved leading theorists: Michael Foucault, Judith Butler, Eve Kosofsky Sedgwick and others. This discourse centered on the way that knowledge of sexuality was constructed through the use of language. Heteronormativity was the main focus of this discourse, whereby heterosexuality was viewed as "normal" and any deviations, such as homosexuality, as labeled as abnormal or "queer."

Queer theory is derived largely from post-structuralist theory and deconstructionist theory in particular. Beginning in the 1970s, a range of authors brought a deconstructionist, critical approaches to issues of sexual identity and especially on the construction of a normative "straight" ideology. Queer theorists challenged the validity and consistency of heteronormative discourse and focused to a large degree on non-heteronormative sexualities and sexual practices, breaking down barriers of labels so that the patriarchal language of the predominate discourses could be challenged and reevaluated.

Ecofeminism links ecology with feminism. Ecofeminists see the domination of women as stemming from the same ideologies that bring about the domination of the environment. Patriarchal systems, where men own and control the land are seen as responsible for the oppression of women and destruction of the natural environment. Ecofeminists argue that the men in power control the land, and therefore they are able to exploit it for their own profit and success. In this situation, women are exploited by men in power for their own profit, success, and pleasure, so Ecofeminists might argue that women and the environment are both exploited as passive pawns in the race to domination. Ecofeminists contend that those people in power are able to take advantage of others distinctly because they are seen as passive and rather helpless. Ecofeminism connects the exploitation and domination of women with that of the environment. As a way of repairing social and ecological injustices, ecofeminists feel that women must work towards creating a healthy environment and ending the destruction of the lands that most women rely on to provide for their families.

Before one can go about theorizing about the gender performativity of werewolves, first one must understand that gender discourses are socially constructed. Under an essentialist view that there is an absolute "femaleness" (and "maleness"), taking the contemporary rules for female behavior and applying them to the contemporary, albeit alternate reality makes sense. Also, by looking at werewolves as human first and then animal second, I can comfortably begin to apply human gendered behavior onto the wolf form of the fictionalized individual. Definitions of sex, gender, heteronormativity must first be discussed so that the discussion can be clearly understood.

Sex refers to biological differences, while gender refers to the cultural construction of masculine and feminine behaviors. Sex is based on chromosomes XX or XY as well as on internal and external sexual organs and the Man and Woman/male-bodied and female-bodied individuals. Gender stereotypes are oversimplified, but strongly held ideas of the expected behaviors of men and women. Gender stereotypes are based on the expectations for how male-bodied and female-bodied individuals "should" behave in one's culture.

Adrienne Rich suggests that we exist in a paradigm of compulsory heterosexuality that is a major organizing principle in our culture (Rich 241). She asks that we look at heterosexuality as being historically situated (an idea echoed by Foucault), yet constantly reinforced by a culture that rewards individuals who fail to challenge the rules. Monique Wittig challenges notions of heteronormativity by asking what defines a woman (Wittig 103) by challenging us to look outside of the limitations put on identity by western culture. One may think that looking at werewolves, who exist outside of the "norms", might be freed from social mores, but my research shows that this is not always the case.

From the time that humans stood upright we have been in a battle of survival, as both predator and prey. We have had to out think our competitors for food, resources, and living space. One of those fiercest competitors has always been the wolf. A creature that to the mindset of the people of Medieval Europe was an animal that thought with the cunningness of humans and the fierceness of demons. The wolf held no reservation about killing humans and their stock as a source of food. Fear of these animals colored local folklore throughout Europe and painted the wolf as a beast spat up from Hell itself and was capable of anything. Stories of werewolves as mindless human/animal murderers served as both a structured social warning and community solidifier for generations.

Stories of the big, bad wolf comfortably placed people together with each other against the "wilds" of our animalistic nature, the environment and its inhabitants. We were safe against the "others", us against them. The image of the wolf remained this way almost until their near extinction in North America. Only when the wolf became one of us, a fragile being in need of help, did the illusion of the beast began to melt. After the North American Timber Wolf was placed on the endangered species list in 1974, multiple, serious studies as well as reevaluations on previous studies into their behavior and lives were conducted revealing a truly different animal.

In 1963 a book by the name of *Never Cry Wolf* written by Canadian author Farley Mowat, lent the public a glance at a previously unknown world of wolf life. Written from a perspective of empathy for the wolf, people began to realize these are not vicious animals with a hell-bent agenda on destroying all humans, but a creature that lived, died and loved. The books influence spanned across Canada and the United States to Russia, where the book was used as a propaganda piece for disarming militant extremists (Geist 14).

At the same time this book accounting the private lives of wolves was written, Betty Friedan's *The Feminine Mystique* (1963) was published, baring the soul of the woman's plight for the world to see. Together these two books threaded together the image of the wolf with women's rights and women's spirituality. Friedan's call for action among all women paralleled the call of animal rights activists for the retelling of the wolf's long neglected tale: The wolf's fight for survival mirrored women's fights for equality. The image of the wolf started to become associated with women's activism, along with the spirituality and conservation message being sent by popular culture of the seventies. The free spirit image of the wolf, backed up by blossoming field research into the wolf behavior, cemented the icon as a deeply spiritually being, strongly connected to the Earth, which laid the ground for works like that of Clarissa Pinkola Estes' *Women Who Run with the Wolves.*

Since the 1970's, the revamping of the lupine image had taken on a more spiritual tone, morphing from a perilous monster into an Earth-wizened creature with characteristics that Americans as a whole, valued. America had just lost its incursion into Vietnam, President John F. Kennedy, Martin Luther King, Jr. and Senator Robert Kennedy had all been assassinated in the span of five years, and faith in the government seemed to be fracturing under political and economic stresses, such as the Watergate scandal. The flower child movement of free love and equality began to falter as stories of dissention, crime and civil unrest seemed to put the United States under an overarching stress of unrest and unease. The comfortable American lifestyle was slipping away. It appeared to this writer that we as a people sought something that was now being revealed to us via the now endangered wolf. A set of subconscious ideals that were now being represented, strong leadership with a rigidly structured hierarchy, monogamous relationships that last a life time, communal and familial bonds that are near supernatural in its strengths were now there for a public that felt that those very aspects were slipping away from them in a world of concrete and commerce. Americans seemed to have become the outsider seeing into their lives. From my perspective, it would appear that as the wolf changes shape from nefarious to noble, so too do our reasons for seeking them out and embracing them. From the first time we saw ourselves as "Othered" or

"Outsider" on the outside looking in at the wolf's life, we wanted the things that these creatures had.

In her book *Women Who Run with the Wolves*, Clarissa Pinkola Estes explores this as the 'wild woman' archetype. She draws a direct parallel between the subjugating of women with environmental destruction, stating like wildlife and wild lands, "the spiritual lands of Wild Woman have been plundered or burnt, dens bulldozed, and natural cycles forced into unnatural rhythms to please others" (Pinkola Estes 3). When women surrender their creative lives, allow their spirit to be brutalized, their sexuality suppressed, they suffer from a deadening of the soul that makes it difficult for them to function fully. Their intuition dulls, and they no longer "run with the wolves": they become broken. Like the greyhound at the track, they may appear to be moving fast and free, but indeed they are little more than moneymakers or a means to an end for their human, and often male, counterparts, with their life spirits drained away until they are hollow physical shells. One way that Pinkola Estes suggests women can reconnect with their feminine spirit is in the form of the Divine Feminine; by connecting with the Primeval Mother, which is a primal force that can be easily identified with a specific primal animal: the wolf.

Fast-forward to the 20th century and the decade of change that was the 1970s. At this time, there was a distinct shift in the discourses of what western culture defines as "horror." Unlike the past, where people genuinely feared the unknown monster in the woods, in the 1970s, reality was scary enough. Interestingly, with the socio-political upheaval in the United States, this was also a time when fictionalized horror novels shifted to show the former "monster" as a misunderstood victim, if not a hero. Anne Rice's groundbreaking *Interview with the Vampire* was published in 1976, focusing on the human within the monster. It was only a matter of time before the formerly lambasted werewolf was reexamined in a similar way. It is in the novel, *Wolfen*, a 1978 horror story by Whitley Strieber, where we fine the center of the book shown through the plight of the intelligent city dwelling wolves and their survival. This piece marks on of the first tales that show the wolf (and shapeshifters) not as a human cautionary tale, but one of conservation. The American audience was clearly ready to reexamine werewolves in multiple media, including movies and television.

In the short-lived television series *Wolf Lake* (2001-2002), the town of Wolf Lake, Oregon is populated by a group of close knit shapeshifters who live along side humans that are friends or loved ones of the shapeshifters. The society of Wolf Lake has each female bodied person, in human form, take on subordinate jobs, positions within the cities commerce and day to day routines. Male members of Wolf Lake have decidedly more masculine jobs, sheriff, mayor bar tender and the like; however, when Vivian Cates takes over as Mayor or pack Alpha, her social scripting changes with her job. Social scripting theory points to the fact that much of sexual behavior seems to follow a script. Society determines appropriate behavior and the meanings attached to those behaviors. Scripts for sexual activity and behaviors are generally markedly different for males and females in all cultures (Wiederman 496).

In this series one of the predominate themes is the initiation into the "pack" with the onset of puberty and first sexual intercourse to induce the first "change" in a focus and controlled environment. For this paper, I viewed all 9 extant episodes of *Wolf Lake* and discovered that both male and female character in the series perform hyper-sexualized gendered behaviors only in the characters human form and, which Butler says: 'There is no gender identity behind the expressions of gender…identity is performativity constituted by the very 'expressions' that are said to be its results" (Gender Trouble 25). In other words, gender is a performance; it's what you do at particular times, rather than a universal that represents who you are. This fits perfectly as gender is only "performed" while in human form, not in wolf form in the series of *Wolf Lake.*
In the show, the female characters, move in sexualized manners, while males stride from place to place in a seemingly over confident manner. This "machismo" is evident when male characters interact with female characters. Machismo itself derives from Spanish macho, coming from the Latin *masculus* "male [animal]" or, when used metaphorically, "masculine" or "very masculine." Tyler Creed, played by Scott Bairstow, is a prime example of this predominate attitude. Creed's machismo, however, melts away in wolf form. Although vicious and knowingly hunts humans, his performed "machismo" is not present while Creed is within the pack formation.

The main female characters (other than Sofia Donner, daughter of the shapeshifter sheriff and human, therefore a possible future initiate) dress to specifications indicative of the male gaze theory: Low cut blouses, exposed mid-drifts and short skirts exposing their legs above the knee. As the show progresses, Sophia, begins to be seen with a more sexualized wardrobe, once she starts to exhibit signs of her impeding transformation as well as social pressure from the local teens who all have transformed. Conversely, males dress in either impeccable suits or form fitting t-shirts and tight pants, accentuating their penises and physical prowess, but still fully clothed.

West and Zimmerman have argued that we perform our gender and that we are accountable to one another for our gender roles, stating that "gender itself is constructed through interactions" (West and Zimmerman 129). These control mechanisms are culturally and historically embedded, with the most dominant institutions or individuals "making the rules" and also holding every individual accountable to them every day. Anyone who departs from the social structure may be considered to be an outcast or deviant. In the series *Wolf Lake*, accountability in their human form is at utmost importance as they must protect the identities of the shapeshifting citizens. They answer to any transgressions to the packs alpha, Willard Cates a male, however Willard dies and is soon replaced by his wife, Vivian. Although in human forms the pack resisted her vie for the alpha seat, but in wolf form she protected the pack and was unanimously declared "Alpha."

The character of Vivian Cates (portrayed by Sharon Lawrence) is seen as a promiscuous, underhanded vixen that seems superficial until the time of need. At the time of her ascension to Alpha, her manor of dress (in human form) changed dramatically to the attire of shrewd business woman. Vivian (the human character) changes according to what is expected of her, moving from tramp to savvy business woman, however as she shifts into her canid form, her likeness does not change from episode to episode. If fact she become indistinguishable from the rest of her pack. Unless you knew which wolf was which based solely on the color of their coat, there was no distinction portrayed amongst the wolves in the wolf pack in *Wolf Lake*. There was no physical indicator as to "who" was in charge or what position they held. The pack of wolves moves in an out of town, without the viewer knowing the genders of any of the wolves.

When the viewer sees the pack interact with one another outside of their performative gendered human forms, positioning inside the unit as a whole lends no indicators as to who each one of the wolves are, either male or female. The animal beings a solidarity against the outside world encroachers, gender politics are washed away for the betterment of the whole. The pack works together, feeds together and are universally loved together, even when their human halves may get bogged down in arguments or political hierarchies.

By shedding off their skin as well as the "act" of being human, the shapeshifters of the television series *Wolf Lake* morph into the truly queer being of werewolf. In werewolf form, they epitomize the ideology of the queer theorists, an androgynous being that is strong, united and safe. They achieve this in a fictional setting doing the seemingly unattainable: becoming genderless and becoming "queer."

I argued that the characters portrayed on the television program *Wolf Lake* have been portrayed in a hyper-heteronormative fashion when in "human" form, but when they transformed into their "beast" form, they shed their idea of gender performativity and slip into a "queer" existence by being completely gender free, even to the point of lacking the defined gender characteristics associated with the western ideals of masculine and feminine. To me there cannot be a purer form of a "queer" existence, regardless of constructed gender stereotypes. The citizens of Wolf Lake, while in wolf form, live this existence with only the social more being "the good of the pack, not the individual." Isn't that what queer theorist strive for: betterment of the community as a whole?

Women's spirituality, the history of the wolf in popular culture and how these two fit together was barely grazed but I feel that it needed to be mentioned and perhaps delved into further in another project. I realize I have touched on many different areas of interest in this paper, I had to change mid-research to a different topic, that although is of interest to me, held a different path than what I wanted to look at. More than anything, this paper has helped to solidify my own understandings of how the ideas of "performativity", "queer" and "feminist theory" will work with my own research in the future, and for that alone, this was a successful project. As a bisexual, half-Native American woman existing in marginalized spaces, I am starting to understand why I identify so readily with the werewolf, who exists in their own duality.

Work Cited

Baring-Gould, Sabine. The Book of Werewolves. New York: Dover, 1865-2006.

Barry, John and Marianne Hester et. al. "Witchcraft in Early Modern Europe." Cambridge: Cambridge University Press, 1996.

Bordo, Susan. "The Body and the Reproduction of Femininity: A Feminist Appropriation of Foucault." Gender/Body/Knowledge: Feminist Reconstructions of Being and Knowing. Eds. Alison M. Jaggar and Susan R. Bordo. New Brunswick: Rutgers UP, 1989. 13-33.

Butler, Judith. Gender Trouble. New York: Routledge, 1999.

----. "Imitation and Gender Subordination." The Lesbian and Gay Studies Reader. Ed. Henry Abelove et al. New York: Routledge, 1993. 307-320.

Colman, Loren and Jerome Clark. Cryptozoology A-Z: The Encyclopedia of Loch Monsters, Sasquatch, Chupacabras and other Authentic Mysteries of Nature. New York: Fireside, 1999.

Crawley, Sara et al. Gendering Bodies. Lanham, MA: Rowman and Littlefield, 2008.

de Beauvoir, Simone. "Introduction" to the Second Sex. The Second Wave Reader in Feminist Theory. Ed. Linda Nicholson. New York: Routledge, 1997. 11-18.

Fedigan, Linda Marie. "The Changing Role of Women in Models of Human Evolution." Annual Review of Anthropology. (1986) 15:25-66.

Hamel, Frank. Werewolves, Bird-Women, Tiger-men and other human animals. New York: Dover Publishing, 1915-2007.

Hollows, Joanne. Feminism, Femininity and Popular Culture. Manchester, UK: Manchester University Press, 2000.

Lorber, Judith. "The Social Construction of Gender." Women's Voices, Feminist Visions. Ed. Susan M. Shaw and Janet Lee. NY: McGraw-Hill, 2007.

Mowat, Farley. "Never Cry Wolf: Amazing True Story of Life Among Arctic Wolves" NY: Time Warner Trade Publishing, 1963

Mulvey, Laura. "Visual Pleasure and Narrative in Cinema." Feminist Film Theory: A Reader. Ed. Sue Thornham. NY: NYU Press, 2006[1999]. 58-69.

Pinkola Estes, Clarissa. "Women Who Run with the Wolves." New York: Ballantine Bertelsmann, 1996[1992].

Rich, Adrienne. "Compulsory Heterosexuality and Lesbian Existence." The Lesbian and Gay Studies Reader. Ed. Henry Abelove et al. New York: Routledge, 1993. 227-254

Sharpe, James. "Witchcraft in Early Modern England." London: Pearson Education, 2001.

Summers, Montague." The Werewolf in Lore and Legend." Minola: Dover, 2003[1933].

West, Candace and Don H. Zimmerman. "Doing Gender." Gender and Society. Vol. 1, No. 2 (June 1987): 125-151.

Wiederman, Michael. "The Gendered Nature of Sexual Scripts." The Family Journal, Vol. 13, No. 4, 496-502. Sage Publications, 2005.

Wittig, Monique. "One is Not Born a Woman." The Lesbian and Gay Studies Reader. Ed. Henry Abelove et al. New York: Routledge, 1993. 103-109.

Wolf Crossing. 2007. The University of Calgary. 26 April 2009 http://wolfcrossing. org/blog/wp-content/uploads/2007/10/carnegie-no1.pdf>.

Wolf Lake: The Complete Series. Sci-Fi Channel. January-February 2009.

4

WHEN THE AUTUMN MOON IS BRIGHT:
AN EXAMINATION INTO IDENTITY, TRANSFORMATION, AND COMING OUT AS A WEREWOLF

She who runs with wolves: the words conjure images of a wild woman running scantily clad through the forest with a large canid loping beside her, wild and free. Perhaps that is what I feel like at times, nearly naked and my companions are animals, free from the social obligations that I adhere to just for the sake of being accepted, conformist…ignored. Since this assignment was to write about anything that I wanted, and apply feminist theory and research methods, I decided to do just that in the form of an autoethnographic research paper that will utilize content analysis of selected pieces of film, folklore and literature to illustrate femininity, identity and the monstrous beauty of duality.

Before we can explore werewolves, you first have to know something about me; I am a Native American who passes as white and a bisexual woman who passes as straight or bisexual woman who passes as gay depending on your perspective. I am a transitional person, multifaceted to the point of near obsession with one thing: the fictional (or not so fictional) beings of werewolves. This human/nonhuman identity is the personification of the physical and emotional reality I live with every day. White/not white, straight/not straight, hairy/not hairy…the duality is a key ingredient to Sally. Not only is duality key, but also my identity as a woman and how my monstrous body is perceived within my society and my own mind is significant to understanding who I am. So logically, I have drawn a line connecting myself and my subject…werewolves. Like it or not, I study werewolves, shapeshifters, skinwalkers and their surrounding folklore. Could there be a strong thread that links folklore and personal identity? Perhaps I will discover what it is to be human, by being werewolf.

This paper will examine two aspects; one is the metamorphosis from human to beast within the context of folklore/films and literature, and the other is an analysis of the female werewolf as a symbol that correlates the parallels between what is it to be a woman in contemporary western culture and the mythos of the werewolf. Then with this adoption practice in mind, I will move on to the interpretations of werewolf imagery in the media as a reflection of feminist theory superimposed upon film in dramatized reality.

Television and films allow us to journey to idealized worlds where a trained eye can read into them meanings never intended by the filmmaker, just as real-life scenarios are interpreted by legions of theorists looking for meaning in words from print or the sounds of disembodied voices across the airwaves, hope hidden behind lyrics of songs and other devices, just as academics seek meaning in the words of their peers. Whether to argue against a statement or idea to find validations for their own feelings, theory of week or personal crusade or to add a missing piece of substance, writers often seek to better themselves or the world around them though their own interpretive means.

Western cultural constructs cite childbirth and motherhood, as well as menstruation, as hallmarks of femininity and the badge of "true" womanhood. Although feminist scholars, such as Monique Wittig and Simone de Beauvoir have long since disbanded the notion of womanhood as solely linked to the ability to give birth, the idea seems to linger. However, the question pertaining to actual identity of "woman" is vast. Each person has a definition and experience to validate the definition; so, to begin with, I am going to discuss what it means to be a woman. In "The Monstrous Feminine", Barbara

Creed challenges this patriarchal viewpoint by arguing that the prototype of all definitions of the monstrous is the female reproductive body and that man fears woman as castrator, rather than as castrated (44). The act of "other" removing a perceived object of power that is physical is horrifying. Because woman is other or "not" man she cannot be castrated, and never know the emotional, physical and psychological of castration.

In Simone de Beauvoir's "Introduction" to *The Second Sex*, the author attempts to analyze the very meaning of what it is to be "woman" through biology, psychoanalysis and historical materialisms and how "feminine" has been fashioned from man to "other" women so the hierarchy of our society is firmly engrained (11). What is it to be woman? According to de Beauvoir, "Males and females are two types of individuals which are differentiated within a species for the function of reproduction; they can be defined only correlatively. But first it must be noted that even the division of a species into two sexes is not always clear-cut" (12). De Beauvoir then states that first she must begin by stating "I am a woman" and by that preliminary answer is significant, as all further discussion will directly relate to that statement (12). A man does not say this. This alone says that all proper discussion or viewpoints that are normal and expected are male based and women are secondary, an exception to "the rules" of common communication. Woman is in a separate category and thus "othered", an outsider in which translation is necessary to continue. This othering is the viewpoint in which I will analyze the following cinematic representations of gendered performance as I see them in the various films and televisions series I previously mentioned, also it is a viewpoint from which I, myself, am associated with and which I take very personally.

Feminists have taken many different approaches to the analysis of cinema. These include discussions of the function of women characters film narratives or in particular genres, such as film noir, where a woman character can often be seen to embody a subversive sexuality that is dangerous to men and is ultimately punished with death. (Clover 163) In considering the way that films are put together, many feminist film critics, such as Laura Mulvey, have pointed to the "male gaze" that predominates in classical Hollywood film making (67). Using various film techniques, such as a reverse shot, the viewer is led to align herself with the point of view of a male protagonist. Notably, women function as objects of this gaze far more often than as proxies for the spectator (Mulvey 68). The perceived ideal of the "perfect" woman is constructed by what men desire. Women tend to enforce the standard via competition for male attention, perpetuating a false identity and thus false human.

Before one can go about theorizing about the gender performativity of werewolves, first one must understand that gender discourses are socially constructed. Under an essentialist view that there is an immutable, innate and trans-historical "femaleness" (and "maleness"), taking the contemporary rules for female behavior and applying them to the contemporary, alternate reality makes sense. Also, by looking at werewolves as human first and then animal second, I can comfortably begin to apply human gendered behavior onto the wolf form of the *fictionalized* individual. Definitions of sex, gender, and heteronormativity must first be discussed so that the discussion can be clearly understood.

Sex refers to biological differences, while gender refers to the cultural construction of masculine and feminine behaviors. Sex is based on chromosomes XX or XY as well as on internal and external sexual organs and the Man and Woman/male-bodied and female-bodied individuals. Gender stereotypes are oversimplified but strongly held ideas of the expected behaviors of men and women. Gender stereotypes are based on the expectations for how male-bodied and female-bodied individuals "should" behave in one's culture.

My own perceptions of my body with regards to my culture could be best described as fractured and complicated. Fill with duality that would make a philosopher's head swim in delirium, so I could simple state why I liken to lycans.

I utilized my anthropological skills of analyzing people objectively and began observing my own behaviors, responses, rituals and physical changes based on photographs past and present as well as the handy mirror. Knowing a background behavioral conditioning had taken place with the ten years at Walt Disney World with the company standard of body image being one of competition and detrimental rewards, I utilized that knowledge as a base for behavioral reactions that would explain a perceived violent reaction or when reaction should have been provoked but none was. Disney fucked me up, or rather the subject.

I began with the mundane, what clothes do I wear and why. The standard form of dress is comprised of jeans and a t-shirt. Rugged and hardy, the no-nonsense clothing is made for easy wear, removal and care. Shoes (if there were any) were generally Birkenstocks, again rugged and easy to wear, remove and care for. My hair is long and wild, braided only to keep from tangling at night and no styling really whatsoever. My manner of outwardly appearance is not what is called "popular" by any means; it has been called "functional." My actual physical body is one that is often looked upon as undesirable. I am 6-foot-tall large bodied woman, an imposing force to be faced with. I have been told too many times to count, that "I would be so pretty if I lost some weight..." And people would so nice if they weren't such assholes, but I digress. Americans have a skewed perception of beauty that in reality does not exist. Like the werewolf, and unlike other monsters, I different enough to be abject but not quite abject enough to put down. By using the comparison of my own body to that of lycans or werewolves the similarities are found to be interestingly similar.

Polycystic ovarian syndrome or PCOS has done some pretty strange things to my body, Parts of my female form has expanded in abnormal shaping, I have grown hair in noticeable and socially embarrassing ways. Mood swings equal to PMS style ups and downs have left me an emotional mess. So, what do I see when I look in the mirror? A suddenly misshapen, hairy beast that craves meat and has extreme anger issues once a month...I am by definition...a werewolf. Though I no longer menstruate regularly, the hormonal surges are still very present.

My distorted body image is a strange duality that straddles both fear and fascination, the horrible and desired. The type of horror most applicable to the werewolf narrative is body horror (or what horror scholar Mark Manovich calls "body/horror"). Manovich suggests, "in...films, the monstrous threat is not external but erupts from within the human body, and so challenges the distinction between self and other, inside and outside." (132). Like two sides of the same coin in the werewolf is a kind of dark double:

." . . two competing sides of an individual – normally, one rational and civilized, the other uncontrolled and irrational, often more primal and atavistic. This duality may also represent a conflict between competing sexualities, gender

orientations, repressed desires and their expressions, or may be a more obvious and confrontational antithesis between the powerful and powerless" (133).

This duality is key not only the analyzing the werewolf but also a glimpse into what makes me, the author tick, as well as seeing us and other, animal and human, males and female the binary categories that the majority of Western cultures focuses in on when dealing with mysterious happenings of the body or mind. My power of my size is also a curse in that I no longer fit within popular culture as ideal. I am imposing and command attention, but on the offhand I also am no longer seen as woman (unwoman according to Kristeva) though I still possess the physical attributes, they are distorted to the point of abject.

Body image is an issue for which most American people, especially women can have a pang of familiarity. We, as Americans, are subject to bombardments of media imagery and notion of "the ideal" woman. Designed by the male gaze and perpetuated by our peers the actual ideal woman, has never and will never exist. Although some may argue within religious circles that the Virgin Mary was the ideal, all others pale by comparison. Granted it is hard to live up to the title "Mother of God" but has that ideal changed? Yes, it has, thanks to media and pop culture.

Women are slowly picked apart physically and slowly, over time, our self-esteems are then sold back to us (Wolf 2). Women are held to a physical standard that causes us to unimaginable things to conform to a social ideal. When the natural function of a woman's body occurs, i.e. her menstrual cycle, it is often greeted with shame, disgust and horror.

As a woman, I have grown accustomed to have having my menstrual cycle. Feared in the beginning, the regular timing set a standard within my life in which I could always count on, comforting discomfort (duality) that reminded me of being human and of being a woman. Then one day it all went away. I cannot have children, which by "popular" definition…made me no longer "woman", a fruitful member of society. PCOS has left me adrift within an identity that once supported me, and all my quirky differences. For according to Catherine MacKinnon "'woman' is defined by what male desire requires for arousal and satisfaction and is socially tautologous with 'female sexuality' and 'the female sex"' (161). Now I feel unable to negotiate my own notion of who I am, let alone navigate through society's opinions. A eunuch of the female variety, not threatening and shunned, and undesired (I felt, though no one knew). I made up for it in ferocity and verbal victims. With my own fertility on my mind I began looking at my body and comparing the similarities between it and lycanthrope one night.

In popular culture and in private life, cautionary tales slung between the men of avoiding a woman who is menstruating for fear of bodily harm is often told in a tongue-in-cheek manor in today's society. These tales are often told within the same framework as one would tell a werewolf story around a campfire. A wandering adventurer (hero) bags his prize within a shrouded wooded area, but his life is cut short by one misstep and he fall victim to his own ignorance, felled by a raging, hairy beast out for his blood. Just as a man who traverses life within an urban jungle, finds a perfect wife or partner only to be verbally cut down to size by his own insensitivity to her physical and emotional needs during her menstrual cycle when perhaps her personal grooming, emotional state and physical discomfort have been radically changed from HIS perceived norm resulting in his attack from his mate.

This notion of victim/aggressor dichotomy with regards to menstruation and werewolves intrigued me, so I decided to look at the correlating components of "menstruation" and "werewolf" by conducting an impromptu survey sprung upon my male friends as they sat around playing zombie games, ribbing each other on their lack of sexual prowess and since I have been dubbed "male" by my friends…(although I am clearly feminine) the comfort of not having a "Girl" present lent for honest feedback from "the guys." I asked them a series of questions based on their own experiences with women within their lives…What's happens to women emotionally when they menstruate? What are their impressions of menstruation? Describe their ideas of physical changes that happen to women during menstruation, and finally describe any myths surrounding menstruation they knew to be true. This type of "open ended interview research explores people's views of reality and allows the researcher to generate theory" (Reinharz 18). Additionally, the impromptu casual setting of my open-ended interview research has enabled me to produce "non-standardized information that allows (me) to make full use of differences among people" (Reinharz 18-19).

To the question of "What happens to a woman emotionally when she menstruates?" I was immediately met with exaggerated body language, collective heads shaking in sadness or defeat, defensively crossed arms and immediate response of "They lose their minds" followed by the obligatory slap of understanding on each other's shoulders and subtle communalism by virtue of the mysterious "othered" female. Each of the five captive participants then quickly shared an anecdotal incident of a wife/ sister/ mother/ partner, laughing at each other's unfortunate run-ins with a she-beast. Trying to remain objective, I merely raised an eyebrow and the group of rowdy men who suddenly realized I too was in fact a woman. They immediately hung their heads sheepishly and sat quietly while I took notes. This is when one said, "they turn on ya…like a sheep killin' dog." After a few more nods of agreement, the group settled down. It was not long though before my newly reemerged state of womanhood melted away again and I was once again one of "The Guys" free to listen to their inner world and insights of the mysterious woman.

The question then came of "What happens to a woman physically during menstruation?" which led to "eauws" and "icks" punctuated by grimaces of disgust blossoming around the room. Once the imagery ran from their minds, they began to answer…

"They bleed."

"They bloat, ache are crampy all over."

"Their boobs get bigger."

"They grow mustaches and their leg hair grows faster."

"They eat like ravenous dogs on a bone. Don't know if that's physical though…"

The nodding in agreement ended with a collective knowing that only these men understood, feeling each other's pain. I scribbled notes until one man tried to escape. I stopped him and told him I needed his input or else everything would be skewed. His response was… "God you're mean. Why would you try and stab us?" It took me a second, then with my response: "That was skewed NOT Skewered"—followed with a promise of Dr. Pepper and pizza—they all sat through the rest of my questions.

I then asked, "What is your impression of menstruation?" I had to revise the question as blank stares greeted me. I asked, "What would you think about menstruation if it happened to you?" Again the "eauws" and "grosses" were followed by something I did not expect. "I would be scared," one man said. "I wouldn't know what was happening." The other men remained silent, trying to grasp the notion and not wanting to admit their true reasoning until one by one each would conclude the same…fear. So, I concluded the question session with "What Myths about menstruation do you know to be "true"?" A few seconds of silence met with a borage of answers,

"Menstrual blood stains more than regular blood" (new one I would have to look up).

"All women craves [sic] meat on their period" (not true, but hey I did).

"Don't know how women can lose so much blood and not be weaker."

"No swimming while on your period."

I did not debunk their myths…in fact I meant not to until the second part of their questionnaire, the one that was going to take place after food, drink and a bit of zombie killing to wash all the girly thoughts of feelings and menstruation out of their minds. The idea was to conduction this second portion of the questionnaire after activities that would relieve the pressure and fear of menstruation. Which each leapt at the chance, their comfort zone had been breached and solace amongst pixilated violence elevated that strain. By round two of zombie killing, all previous engagement of the fairer sex had been washed clean…my precious clean slates. At the break I told them I wanted to talk about werewolves. I was greeted with sighs of relief and mock wolf howls to signal their appreciation of not having to sit through another "period" question.

I began with "What myths do you know about werewolves?" It was like I was at a monster connoisseur's convention…

"Well in Medieval Europe werewolves were just stories about poisoned peasants…"

"Depends on the movie…Dog Soldiers vs. The Howling are examples of…"

"In the books by Brian Easton…"

Each man had a point while the other had a counterpoint to whichever "werewolf" event or myth surrounding silver bullets, full moons, curse or birth the first could recount. The list was long and in depth full of resources and follow up information. These men knew far more about fictional beings than they did about the female sex. After thirty minutes of discussion, I corralled them into making a decision down to three things…1) It takes silver to kill a werewolf, (2) A werewolf turns on the full moon of every month, but shapeshifters shift at will and, (3) It is a curse.

The next question was "What would you do if you were infected with Lycanthropy?" Without hesitation, high-fives were slapped around the room, and one by one each answered…

"I would sooo run naked in the woods."

"It would be AWESOME!"

"I would be the master of my domain and pee on everything."

"I would be so feared, no one would fuck with me at work."

The men sat around and theorized about their newfound pack: who of the five would ascend to alpha male within, what territory would be theirs for hunting. and the inevitable claim to mates. Once their grunting and giggling ebbed, my next question was on them: "What physical changes would occur to them as they shifted into werewolves?" Again, the theories ranged from the painful popping and swelling and stretching of the body to the barely noticed shapeshifter transformation rounded the room meeting with point/counterpoint examination. Every werewolf book, film, television show, story and folktale that included transformation scenes was discussed. Once again, the choice had to be narrowed to three…they chose 1) Pain and bleeding because of tissue damage, (2) Grow a fur coat, and (3) Grow bigger. Finally, they all also added that the werewolf, regardless of transformation, had to eat meat to survive…preferably long pig (human), but not always. It was also at this time that the newly dubbed "Alpha Male" began to catch on to the questions, but before he had the chance to tell the group, I interrupted with the final question of the session…" Does the human within remember what the werewolf did when he was transformed?" A collective voice shouted "No" in unison. Then I followed with "Can the man within be held responsible for the werewolf's actions?" This one met with some debate, but it was decided that it was not the fault of the man if the man could not remember, because the beast was in charge. I threw one last question on them, to be answered quickly with one or the other statement, male or female: "Werewolf?" They all answered "Male." Only the "alpha" shook his head and smiled as I smugly gathered my data and thanked each of my friends. After the group disbanded and I stayed behind to talk with "Alpha", he quietly remarked, "Perhaps I should be nicer to my girlfriend during 'that time'..." My response... "Ya think?"

What this impromptu research shows is that the ideas about menstruating women that the men of this group feared were nearly the same as the werewolf ideas they identified with and admired. Several words describing women were linked to a bestial nature, specifically "canine." References to eating of meat, wild temperament and excusable actions were also mentioned. "Alpha" had realized the parallels, but only after prompting, and we both doubted the other members of his "pack" would realize the correlations. The werewolf and women were strongly reinforced by this group of friends, called "The Pack", with just a series of simple questions, yet so vastly treated it was staggering. Barbara Creed would be proud. In Gloria Steinem's piece "*If Men Could Menstruate: Apolitical Fantasy*" she theorized that men would brag about how much and how long their periods were. Sanitary supplies would be federally funded and free and that a boy's onset of menstruation would be cause for celebration into manhood. (262) based the findings from this little experiment; Gloria would have been spot on. Men would not be placed in the abject realm, but in the human realm.

When Barbara Creed expanded upon Kristeva's idea of woman as abject and that abject falls into two categories: excremental (pollution of identity from outside) and menstrual (pollution of identity from within) (Creed 12) the idea of anything was linked back to the female body and was to be feared. According to Julia Kristeva, since the abject is situated outside the symbolic order, a being is forced to face it is an inherently traumatic experience. The idea of abject is the revulsion response to particular stimuli, to place the object of revulsion away from you. As seen with my impromptu experiment, the idea of menstrual blood, hairy women and distorted body ideals are repulsive and shunned. The males giggled and laughed, however their body language spoke volumes. The defensive crossed arms, the standing taller away from the questions about menstruation and their oh-so-willing departure from the subject to that of supernatural beings, zombie killing and self-fantasized bestial natures that remarkably ran parallel to the menstrual cycles of women.

Creed explains how females are often related to the object of horror, be they as the object of horror or the object of the actual horrors' desire/hatred. The conclusion is that through monstrous representations of the female or the Mother, the audience is drawn into viewing them as abject rather than subject or object. (Creed 13)

The lunar cycle and the menstrual cycle of women are so closely linked within the collective psyche of the mass populace the jump from woman to werewolf is barely a jump at all. The word menstruation does after all derive from the Latin word *mensis* meaning month which has the same Indo-European root meaning "the moon" (Izzard 96). So according to my friends in the question session, is menstruation really a curse? Now that I have brought these parallels to their attention, via my questions and "alpha" they merely nod their head and say, "We always knowed [sic] you was a werewolf and you like werewolves…so maybe it's not a curse…for you."

I mentioned before the idea of metamorphosis and the changing from human to wolf or female to wolf as a point of fascination. The notion to change a physical being that represents one ideal to completely change form and represent another is a radical notion that many people have pondered. The chrysalis to moth analogy is popular as this creature represents the very embodiment (in the natural world) of the magical possibilities.

In the short-lived television series *Wolf Lake,* the town of Wolf Lake, Oregon is populated by a group of close knit shapeshifters who live along side humans that are friends or loved ones of the shapeshifters. The society of *Wolf Lake* has each female bodied person, in human form, take on subordinate jobs, positions within the cities commerce and day to day routines. Male members of Wolf Lake have decidedly more masculine jobs, sheriff, mayor bar tender and the like, however when Vivian Cates takes over as Mayor or pack Alpha, her social scripting changes with her job. Social scripting theory points to the fact that much of sexual behavior seems to follow a script. Society determines appropriate behavior and the meanings attached to those behaviors. Scripts for sexual activity and behaviors are generally markedly different for males and females in all cultures (Wiederman 496).

In this series one of the predominate themes is the initiation into the "pack" with the onset of puberty and first sexual intercourse to induce the first "change" in a focus and controlled environment.

For this paper, I viewed all 9 extant episodes of *Wolf Lake* and discovered that both male and female character in the series perform hyper-sexualized gendered behaviors only in the characters human form and, which Butler says: 'There is no gender identity behind the expressions of gender; ... identity is performativity constituted by the very "expressions" that are said to be its results.' (Gender Trouble 25). In other words, gender is a performance; it's what you do at particular times, rather than a universal that represents who you are. This fits perfectly as gender is only "performed" while in human form, not in wolf form in the series of *Wolf Lake*.

In the show, the female characters, move in sexualized manners, while males stride from place to place in a seemingly over confident manner. This "machismo" is evident when male characters interact with female characters. Machismo itself derives from Spanish macho, coming from the Latin *masculus* "male [animal]" or, when used metaphorically, "masculine" or "very masculine." Tyler Creed, played by Scott Bairstow, is a prime example of this predominate attitude. Creed's machismo, however, melts away in wolf form. Although vicious and knowingly hunts humans, his performed "machismo" is not present while Creed is within the pack formation.

The main female characters (other than Sofia Donner, daughter of the shapeshifter sheriff and human, therefore a possible future initiate) dress to specifications indicative of the male gaze theory: Low cut blouses, exposed mid-drifts and short skirts exposing their legs above the knee. As the show progresses, Sophia, begins to be seen with a more sexualized wardrobe, once she starts to exhibit signs of her impeding transformation as well as social pressure from the local teens who all have transformed. Conversely, males dress in either impeccable suits or form fitting t-shirts and tight pants, accentuating their penises and physical prowess, but still fully clothed.

West and Zimmerman have argued that we perform our gender and that we are accountable to one another for our gender roles, stating that "gender itself is constructed through interactions" (West and Zimmerman 129). These control mechanisms are culturally and historically embedded, with the most dominant institutions or individuals "making the rules" and also holding every individual accountable to them every day. Anyone who departs from the social structure may be considered to be an outcast or deviant. In the series

Wolf Lake, accountability in their human form is at utmost importance as they must protect the identities of the shape shifting citizens. They answer to any transgressions to the packs alpha, Willard Cates a male, however Willard dies and is soon replaced by his wife, Vivian. Although in human forms the pack resisted her vie for the alpha seat, but in wolf form she protected the pack and was unanimously declared "Alpha."

The character of Vivian Cates portrayed by Sharon Lawrence is seen as a promiscuous, underhanded vixen that seems superficial until the time of need. At the time of her ascension to Alpha, her manor of dress (in human form) changed dramatically to the attire of shrewd business woman. Vivian human character changes according to what is expected of her, moving from tramp to savvy business woman, however as she shifts into her canid form, her likeness does not change from episode to episode. If fact she become indistinguishable from the rest of her pack. Unless you knew which wolf was which based solely on the color of their coat, there was no distinction portrayed amongst the wolves in the wolf pack in *Wolf Lake*. There was no physical indicator as to "who" was in charge or what position they held. The pack of wolves moves in an out of town, without the viewer knowing the genders of any of the wolves.

When the viewer sees the pack interact with one another outside of their performative gendered human forms, positioning inside the unit as a whole lends no indicators as to who each one of the wolves are, either male or female. The animal beings a solidarity against the outside world encroachers, gender politics are washed away for the betterment of the whole. The packs works together, feeds together and are universally loved together, even when their human halves may get bogged down in arguments or political hierarchies.

The shedding off of the "act" of the human form the shapeshifters live in the television series *Wolf Lake* into the truly queer being of werewolf sought after is by queer theorists, an androgynous, being that is strong, united and safe. They achieved this in a fictional setting doing the seemingly unattainable…by becoming genderless, the very meaning of becoming "queer." I argued that the characters portrayed on the television program *Wolf Lake* have been portrayed in a hyper-heteronormative fashion when in "human" form, but when they transformed into their "beast" form, they shed their idea of gender performativity and slip into a "queer" existence by being completely gender free, even to the point of lacking the defined gender characteristics associated with the western ideals of masculine and feminine. To me there cannot be a purer form of a "queer" existence, regardless of constructed gender stereotypes, the citizens of Wolf Lake, while in wolf form, live this existence with only the social moiré of "the good of the pack" not the individual. Isn't that what queer theorist strive for: betterment of the community as a whole?

Not all change is good, at least not in the eyes of the public. The notion of change can be frightening and In Hamish Thompson's article "She's Not Your Mother Anymore, She's a Zombie", Thompson argues that psychological continuity in zombies permits moral devaluation of zombies and thus their personal identity is compromised allowing we the survivors a moral ground to destroy the monstrous body (28). With their identity forever gone the only thing left to do is put down the body, permanently killing it by decapitation or immolation. This interpretation dealing with the continuity of body, mind and soul plays out in with the idea that once a person has been infected with lycanthropy, their identity has been forever changed. A cure is seemingly on an option and ultimate destruction of the new physical form must be played out. In the 1981 film *The Howling*, Television reporter Karen White is confronted by a colony of werewolves living within the Unites States, trying to maintain an existence that does not include killing people. We follow her toils and tribulations throughout the film, becoming her companion alongside, however, with her ultimate infection of Lycanthropy, she transforms in front of the television cameras...wanting her partner to kill her to prove of the werewolf being and body does exist. Even though there can be a life for her with her new-found hairiness once a month, she chooses death over the physical aberration. We, the viewer, never question our heroine's decision and scarcely bat an eye when she has been killed. She has become abject an object to cast far away from us no matter the previous relationship. Countless other werewolf characters have met the same fate. Death because of change.

In his article "Zombie Gladiators" by Dale Jacquette, argues the subtle differences of *Automata*: the automaton and the *Conscios*: the real person (105). The philosophical zombie (or automation) is only recognizable by a small mark on the back of the neck but is otherwise indistinguishable from humans. Each performs identically and appears to have an identity, yet only conscios actually HAVE identity, while the automata merely perform it, giving the *conscios* license to deal with them as seen fit. Just as Some Americans turn a blind eye to the treatment of people of larger sizes, this idea of real and not real humans takes for in the treatment of overweight Americans. Because of a singular physical marker, they are targeted as being almost non-human and therefore non-feeling. Subject to ridiculous measures of the public to try and force over weight individual to conform "for their own health" and thus justifying public humiliation, torture and ultimate rejection by that forceful public. This applies to images of the werewolf within the British television series *Being Human* in which the promise of normalcy is sought after by the werewolf George, who is determined to fit into human society by living with other supernatural creatures, Mitchell (vampire) and Annie (ghost) in a flat in Bristol. For his own safety and well-being, George must be locked up once a month to prevent him from killing any humans or prevent humans from killing him. So much is wrapped around his trying to be human that the humans that know simply try to cure the lycanthropy without dealing with the individual, George. George too cannot deal with his otherness and only at the end of series one did he begin to come to grips with his furry nature and begin seeing life as a werewolf is not all bad, just different. In his realization he becomes more human by embracing his werewolf self.

So, it would seem for me as the writer to embrace who I am, a large woman with PCOS, and live by George's example to become human I must embrace my nature. I feel I have done so. With the aid of my werewolf counterparts I feel stronger, better…more natural than before. I touch back to my Native American blood by embracing myself as a skinwalker. Full of changes that are beautiful, powerful and mysterious, though like George, I still struggle with the negotiation of life as a skinwalker living within a very human world with all its trials and tribulations, but then again, being human is the same. Analyzing werewolf and human behavior portrayed in the media and within a closed question session, I learned that the reality of the unknown is scary for a lot of individuals and fear is often met with avoidance, violence and distrust. Why is it that a desired state of being and a loathed state of being can be nearly identical? Duality.

The members of "The Pack" strove to become the one thing that scared them, something mysterious and powerful, they believe it to be werewolves…I believe it to be woman. For me nothing is more those things than woman…So here I am, coming out as a woman, and a werewolf to my classmates and myself.

Works Cited

Badley, Linda. *Film, Horror, and the Body Fantastic*, Contributions to the Study of Popular Culture. Westport: Greenwood Press, 1995.

Balsamo, Anne. *Technologies of the Gendered Body: Reading Cyborg Women.* Durham: Duke University Press, 1996.

Barker, Martin, Ernest Mathijs, and Xavier Mendik. "Menstrual Monsters: The Reception of the Ginger Snaps Cult Horror Franchise." *Film International* 4, no. 21 (2006): 68-77.

Bordo, Susan. *Unbearable Weight: Feminism, Western Culture, and the Body.* 10th Anniversary ed. Berkeley, CA: U. of California Press, 2003.

---. "The Body and the Reproduction of Femininity: A Feminist Appropriation of Foucault." Gender/Body/Knowledge: Feminist Reconstructions of Being and Knowing. Eds. Alison M. Jaggar and Susan R. Bordo. New Brunswick: Rutgers UP, 1989. 13-33.

Butler, Judith. *Gender Trouble.* New York: Routledge, 1999.

----. "Imitation and Gender Subordination." *The Lesbian and Gay Studies Reader.* Ed. Henry Abelove et al. New York: Routledge, 1993. 307-320.

Carroll, Noel. "Nightmare and the Horror Film: The Symbolic Biology of Fantastic Beings." *Film Quarterly* 34, no. 3 (1981): 16-25.226

Clark, Elizabeth. "Girl Werewolves Onscreen! A Master's Thesis Research Project." livejournal.com, http://girl-werewolves. livejournal.com/.

Clover, Carol. *Men, Women, and Chain Saws: Gender in the Modern Horror Film.* Princeton, NJ: Princeton University Press, 1993.

Cohen, Jeffrey Jerome. "Monster Culture (Seven Theses)." In *Monster Theory: Reading Culture*, edited by Jeffrey Jerome Cohen, 3-20. Minneapolis: University of Minnesota Press, 1997.

Craig, Robert J. "Howling at the Moon: The Origin Story in Werewolf Cinema." *Popular Culture Review* 17, no. 1 (2006): 31-39.

Creed, Barbara. *The Monstrous-Feminine: Film, Feminism, Psychoanalysis.* London: Routledge, 1993.

---. "Dark Desires: Male Masochism in the Horror Film." In *Screening the Male: Exploring Masculinities in Hollywood Cinema*, edited by Steven Cohan and Ina Rae Hark, 118-33. New York: Routledge, 1993.

De Beauvoir, Simone. "Introduction" The Second Wave: A reader in Feminist Theory: Ed. Linda Nicholson. New York: Routledge. 1997.

du Coudray, Chantal Bourgault. "Upright Citizens on All Fours: Nineteenth-Century Identity and the Image of the Werewolf." *Nineteenth-Century Contexts* 24, no. 1 (2002): 1-16.

---. "A Manifesto for Werewolves: What the Cyborgs Didn't Tell Us." *Paradoxa* 17 (2003): 151-75.

Haraway, Donna. "A Cyborg Manifesto: Science, Technology, and Socialist- Feminism in the Late Twentieth Century." In *Simians, Cyborgs and Women: The Reinvention of Nature*, 149-81. New York: Routledge, 1991.

Hollows, Joanne. *Feminism, Femininity and Popular Culture*. Manchester, UK: Manchester University Press, 2000.

Izzard, John. *Werewolves*. NY. Octopus Publishing Group, 2009.

Jancovich, Mark. "General Introduction." In Horror, the Film Reader, edited by Mark Jancovich. London: Routledge, 2002.

Jacquette, Dale. "Zombie Gladiators." The Undead and Philosophy. Ed. Richard Greene and K. Silem Mohammad. Peru, IL: Open Court, 2006. 105-118.

Larkin, William S. "Res Corporealis: Persons, Bodies and Zombies." The Undead and Philosophy. Ed. Richard Greene and K. Silem Mohammad. Peru, IL: Open Court, 2006. 15-26.

Lorber, Judith. "The Social Construction of Gender." *Women's Voices, Feminist Visions*. Ed. Susan M. Shaw and Janet Lee. NY: McGraw-Hill, 2007.

MacKinnon, Catherine. "Sexuality." The Second Wave: A Reader in Feminist Theory: Ed. Linda Nicholson. New York: Routledge. 1997.

Mulvey, Laura. "Visual Pleasure and Narrative in Cinema." *Feminist Film Theory: A Reader*. Ed. Sue Thornham. NY: NYU Press, 2006[1999]. 58-69.

Nielsen, Bianca. ""Something's Wrong, Like More Than You Being Female": Transgressive Sexuality and Discourses of Reproduction in 'Ginger Snaps'." *thirdspace* 3, no. 2 (2004): 55-69.

O'Donnell, Elliot. *Werewolves*. Maryland. Wildside Press. 2008

Otten, Charlotte F. *A lycanthropy Reader: Werewolves of Western Culture*. New York. Syracuse University Press. 1986.

Steiger, Brad. *The Werewolf Book: The Encyclopedia of Shape-Shifting Beings.* Detroit: Visible Ink Press, 1999.

Steinem, Gloria. "If Men could Menstruate: A Political Fantasy." Women's Health. Dubuque: Kendall/Hunt Publishing. (1978) 2009

Thompson, Hamish. "`She's Not Your Mother Anymore, She's a Zombie!': Zombies, Value, and Personal Identity." The Undead and Philosophy.   Ed. Richard Greene and K. Silem Mohammad. Peru, IL: Open Court, 2006. 27-38.

Wiederman, Michael ."The Gendered Nature of Sexual Scripts." *The Family Journal,* Vol. 13, No. 4, 496-502. Sage Publications, 2005

West, Candace and Don H. Zimmerman. "Doing Gender." Gender and Society. Vol. 1,No. 2. June 1987): 125-151

Wolf, Naomi. The Beauty Myth: How Images of Beauty Are Used Against Women. Harper Perennial; Reprint edition (September 24, 2002).

5

"LAST BITCH STANDING": FEMALE WEREWOLVES AS HEROINES, MOTHERS, AND THE "FINAL GIRL"

The mind's eye conjures up many things when different words are spoken. Werewolf immediately brings forth the idea of large bi-pedal beasts with rippling muscles, foaming jaws, massive claws secured upon powerful paws with hair flowing wildly in the light of the full moon. Rarely are werewolves thought of as feminine. Films have begun to change that perception. Female werewolves are becoming more popular and with it more powerful. This paper explores the literal and figurative embodiment of femininity coded within the narratives of werewolf films, specifically where the female werewolf is also the "last bitch standing" at the end. Using theoretical constructs such as *vagina dentata*, the Final Girl and the Monstrous Feminine, I hope to explore how these ideas can be applied to werewolf stories as a genre and female werewolves as a whole. \

By examining films like *The Howling* (1980), *Dog Soldiers* (2002), as well as the sub-story line of the 2007 film *Trick R Treat*, these movies will act as tools to discuss the position of the female werewolves within these films and how they fit the criteria of heroine, mother, the "Final Girl" and how these were-women are both seductive and truly horrifying. By inverting Carol Clover's argument about the "final girl" completely, I will show how this position is both abject and seductive to the viewing audience. In each film we are shown beautiful young women, who happen to be werewolves that proceed to commit acts that we presume to be horror, but do so because their homes are terrorized, their loved ones are at risk, and/or simply to provide for their packs.

I will argue that, via the invasion narrative, these women's home territories were invaded, and they took action to preserve their families and their ways of life. Both Marsha and Megan face the horror that comes into their homes; they fight and ultimately defeat the monster...humans. Laurie, stalks a threat to her pack and her community, a human with bad intentions. The films' final battles and final scenes will be used to illustrate the victorious females (but not necessarily happy outcome) and how these women/werewolves are portrayed as simultaneously repulsive and seductive. These sympathetic monsters are more than just cursed humans, but they are in fact Alphas or in the case of Laurie, soon to be Alpha, of their packs and their power, beauty and unrestrained brutality in defense of their packs are the both intoxicating and frightening for viewers.

When one thinks of "werewolves" the word usually connotes male/masculinity, especially in American Horror Films. Before one can go about theorizing about the gender performativity of werewolves, first one must understand that gender discourses are socially constructed. Under an essentialist view that there is an immutable, innate and transhistorial "femaleness" (and "maleness"), taking the contemporary rules for female behavior and applying them to the contemporary, alternate reality makes sense. Also, by looking at werewolves as human first and then animal second, I can comfortably begin to apply human gendered behavior onto the wolf form of the fictionalized individual. Werewolves are large, muscular, strong, aggressive, and territory, which are all traditionally masculine traits in western culture. Conversely, women are taught to take up less space, to be quiet and demure, to be passive. Werewolves, like western males, are dominant and hierarchical.

Films allow us to journey to idealized worlds, a trained eye can read into them meanings never intended by the filmmaker, just as real life scenarios are interpreted by legions of theorists looking for meaning in words from print or the sounds of disembodied voices across the airwaves, hope hidden behind lyrics of songs and other devices, just as academics seek meaning in the words of their peers. Whether to argue against a statement or idea to find validations for their own feelings, theory of week or personal crusade or to add a missing piece of substance, writers often seek to better themselves or the world around them though their own interpretive means. When studying werewolves, it is necessary to acknowledge a large historical, literary and filmic body of work: the werewolf cannon as it were.

Feminists have taken many different approaches to the analysis of cinema. These include discussions of the function of women characters in particular film narratives or in particular genres, such as film noir, where a woman character can often be seen to embody a subversive sexuality that is dangerous to men and is ultimately punished with death. In considering the way that films are put together, many feminist film critics, such as Laura Mulvey, have pointed to the "male gaze" that predominates in classical Hollywood film making (67) . Through the use of various film techniques, such as a reverse shot, the viewer is led to align herself with the point of view of a male protagonist. Notably, women function as objects of this gaze far more often than as proxies for the spectator (Mulvey 68).

Adrienne Rich suggests that we exist in a paradigm of compulsory heterosexuality that is a major organizing principle in our culture (Rich 241). She asks that we look at heterosexuality as being historically situated (an idea echoed by Foucault), yet constantly reinforced by a culture that rewards individuals who fail to challenge the rules. Monique Wittig and Marilyn Frye both challenge notions of heteronormativity by asking what defines a woman (Wittig 103; Frye 97). Wittig, Frye et al challenge us to look outside of the constraints put on identity by western culture. One may think that a television show or movie set in an alternate reality might be freed from social mores.

The type of horror most applicable to the werewolf narrative is body horror (or what horror scholar Mark Jancovich calls "body/horror") "In these films, the monstrous threat is not external but erupts from within the human body, and so challenges the distinction between self and other, inside and outside." (132). Like two sides of the same coin in the werewolf is a kind of dark double:

". . . two competing sides of an individual – normally, one rational and

civilized, the other uncontrolled and irrational, often more primal and atavistic. This duality may also represent a conflict between competing sexualities, gender orientations, repressed desires and their expressions, or may be a more obvious sand confrontational antithesis between the powerful and powerless"(133)

This duality is key not only the analyzing the werewolf but also a glimpse into what makes me, the author tick, as well as seeing us and other, animal and human, males and female the binary categories that the majority of Western cultures focuses in on when dealing with mysterious happenings of the body or mind.

One of the basic premises of Clover's theory is that audience identification is unstable and fluid across gender lines, particularly in the case of the slasher film. During the final girl's confrontation with the killer, Clover argues, she becomes masculinized through "phallic appropriation" by taking up a weapon, such as a knife or chainsaw, against the killer. According to Clover, these weapons are phallic because they look like dicks and they penetrate.

The myth of the vagina dentata, or vagina with teeth, derives from primitive masculine dreads of the "mysteries" of women and sexual union. It evokes castration anxiety, whereby the man fears loss of the penis during intercourse, and more generally it relates to fears of weakness, impotence, or annihilation by incorporation (connected to unconscious notions of "returning to the womb"). With this in mind the prospect of highly sexualized females that conform to the heteronormative standard in our Western culture, causes a short hiccup in the minds of viewers which seek out the pleasing form only to have it coupled with very imposing and lethal sharp teeth wrapped in velvety lips that draw their attention. The desire to fuck, fight or flight becomes a moment of indecision within the brain that may cause anxiety. The anxiety turns to fear at an increased level once the sex drive is now fueling it and once the scene ends, creates a bigger sense of relief once normalcy returns to the film scenario.

This anxiety ramps up the fear within the viewers psyche that lends to the Freudian stance of fear, that we as viewers enjoy the return to normalcy, I believe that with the added spice of the vagina dentate, the ride up as well as down plays a part or the increased "high" of the control fear of horror movies.

The majority of men seem to believe that women are capable of some degree of evil at some time or the other. In reference to what Freud wrote when he said, "Probably no male being is spared the terrifying shock of threatened castration as the sight of the female genitals." ("Fetishism" by Sigmund Freud, 1927) shows that there is a reference to sex in all things and that there is also a constant battle between the sexes. The idea centers on the female capability of evil quite unparalleled to that of men. Throughout films, especially horror movies of the 1950's and 1960's the monster was almost always a male dominant role with a few exceptions. When the role of the monster is female, there is almost always a male hero who destroys it utterly and usually with very little remorse.

The female werewolf however, represents an aspect of horror to the male viewer by several things. One, the female before him is more powerful, masculine and deadly than he. The she wolf can easily overpower her male victims and by using her most terrifying weapon...her mouth. Like Michael Myers using his phallic knife to enforce his masculinity, Marsha in *The Howling* uses her vagina dentate to do the same. She attacks the male victim, in a sense raping the male and infecting/impregnating him with her bite. She then forces the man, upon the next full moon to do what every man fears...give birth. With his skin tearing and bones moving the male victim literally gives birth to himself as a new creature, an uncontrolled monster. Thus, reversing the comfortable stereotype of male and female in this horror setting, to uncomfortable terror.

The Howling, a werewolf film from 1980, gave us the uber-sexualized "were-oine" Marsha. Marsha wore skin- tight -black leather dress slit as far up as down, waves of flowing raven hair with a silent strength that oozes sex. Marsha is our apex mom, heroine and final girl. She is loving, caring and protective of her pack, she fights through personal hardships to keep the family going and to care for those already in the fold.

When it comes to motherhood, Marsha may not be your conventional June Cleaver, but she does exhibit the qualities one would associate with being a proper mother in a world where you are "othered" by society at large. Marsha cares for her mentally challenged (even for werewolf standards) brother Eddie. When Eddie becomes fixated upon a news reporter, she indulges Eddie and allows him to pursue his "love" interest because of familial love. She does not deny him the chance at happiness nor love but helps him hide from the world outside *the colony*, even though his folly draws attention to their territory. She enlists the aid of her pack to bring

Karen and her husband bill into the pack. Marsha herself starts with a weakened, emasculated Bill to turn first, for he is obviously the beta within their relationship. Bill is a vegetarian, Karen refuses to take his last name in marriage and Karen makes more money than he lending to the notion of many Americans, especially at that time, that although Karen is sweet and soft spoken, she wears the pants in the family. This mentality would be seen as vulnerable by the apex predators such as werewolves as a weakness to exploit, wither for food or familial procreation, Bill was the natural choice. I propose that Marsha is not only a heroine for her pack in a time of need, but also a mother figure to her brother Eddie as well as Bill when she cleans and cooks a killed rabbit for him nurturing his perceived weakened, vegetarian body with a much-needed protein charge. Once bitten and initiated into the pack Bill joins the other bachelor wolves but becomes fiercely protective of his new "mother" when Karen speaks ill of her. This type of devotion to their mothers is often seen in men and not at all unusual, in fact quite normal and expected by western cultural standards.

Finally, Marsha is also a "final girl." Not only does she succeed in removing the threat from her pack and territory, she escapes to continue to bring new life into the pack. At the climax of the film, Marsha stands in a rustic barn surrounded by her pack. As Karen is brought before the pack Marsha stands central and in front of the framed wolves, this illustrates the power of her position, literally, within the pack. When a squabble breaks out, Marsha is quick to discipline the elder wolf and reclaim her authority position immediately. Her alpha status is never challenged again.

In the 2002 film, *Dog Soldiers*, the final werewolf is Megan. Megan is believed to be human, and the sole-survivor of a massive werewolf attack in the Scottish countryside, but in fact she is the alpha female of the pack. Megan tries to get the human soldiers to leave before the pack arrives at the deserted farmhouse where she is living; however, because she is "just a girl" the military dismiss her warnings. The command team sets up a perimeter around the farmhouse to ride out the werewolf attack, unwittingly barricading themselves within the werewolf den, much like the Coopers locking themselves in the basement with Karen in *Night of the Living Dead* (1968): the danger is all around and within the supposedly safe structure.

Megan is revealed when the soldiers realize there is nothing silver in the house. Megan reveals her true self and their chances of survival vanish. She opens the door to the farmhouse as if to run, but she stands on the threshold transforming, with the fully transformed pack behind her. Three soldiers, the only still remaining survivors, who are in the house, slowly realize their predicament. Even though one soldier attacks her by shooting her, she gets up and with her pack, proceeds to kill everyone in the house. Though the home is destroyed presumably taking Megan with it, Sean and Megan's dog leave the final frame of the film, battered and weary.

Although Sean and the family dog are the last to stride out of the home and Megan is presumed dead, victory is in the knowledge that no one will return to the now barren farm for there is no need of its use.

This film is an Invasion Narrative because the victims are secluded in a farmhouse out in the middle of Scotland and the monster is invading a perceived safe space. Megan is the final girl/werewolf because she faces the main intruder and either bites or stabs, but attacks, the invader and facilitates the death of the perceived threat sacrificing her life to do so. It is her homeland, and literally her house, that has been taken over by humans intent on only one thing: destroying her family. When she shifts in the end, she is confronting the soldiers head on, bracing for the imminent attack with her available weapons, her mouth and her claws.

Laurie's role within the Pack in the film *Trick r Treat* is that she is Beta and the last of her pack to mature. How she is "final girl", mother and heroine differs from Marsha and Megan in several ways. She has an androgynous name, but she is hyper-feminized, in contrast to her hyper-sexualized sisters and pack mates. It is her inner strength that marks her as a heroine. She is not a final girl in that all her pack survives, however her drive to protect family traditions is paramount. Her role in the pack is that of Future Alpha / Mother / Nurturer.

Based on Anna Paquin's performance of Laurie, she managed to portray virginal innocence with lethal cunning. She is dressed like Little Red Riding Hood, but just before her shift to werewolf, she loses her cape and shirt, just like Marsha and Megan do before their own shifts. Laurie becomes hairy and toothy, bathed in orange light with blue backlighting, hearkening back to the duality of the film and the duality of werewolves themselves. As werewolves, the women of Laurie's pack are charged with the protection of the surrounding community (from undesired males). Laurie chooses the one man who seemed to be stalking her and ultimately attacks her. By removing this threat as she claims her place in the pack and protects the community.

This paper argues that the depiction of female werewolves in these three films displays characteristic that are often attributed to women being heroines, exemplary mothers, and the "final girl". By inverting Clover's argument completely, I suggest that this position is both abject and seductive to the viewing audience. The audience expects mothers, heroines, and yes, "typical females" when they meet these characters. Instead, in each film, we are shown beautiful young women, who happen to be werewolves that proceed to commit acts that we presume to be horror, but in doing so, they subvert the dominate paradigms for gendered behaviors in American culture, and arguably, in American film.

Works Cited

Carroll, Noel. "Nightmare and the Horror Film: The Symbolic
    Biology of Fantastic Beings." *Film Quarterly* 34, no. 3 (1981): 16-
    25.226

Clover, Carol. *Men, Women, and Chain Saws: Gender in the Modern Horror
    Film.* Princeton, NJ: Princeton University Press, 1993.

Creed, Barbara. *The Monstrous-Feminine: Film, Feminism, Psychoanalysis.*
    London: Routledge, 1993.

---. "Dark Desires: Male Masochism in the Horror Film." In *Screening
    the Male: Exploring Masculinities in Hollywood Cinema*, edited by
    Steven Cohan and Ina Rae Hark, 118-33. New York: Routledge,
    1993.

Dog Soldiers. Dir. Neil Marshall. Perf. Sean Pertwee, Kevin McKidd
    and Emma Cleasby. Artisan, 2002.

Howling, The. Dir. Joe Dante. Perf. Christopher Stone, Dee Wallace,
    Belinda Balaski and Patrick McNee. MGM, 1980.

Jancovich, Mark. "General Introduction." In Horror, the Film
    Reader, edited by Mark Jancovich. London: Routledge, 2002.

Leach, Maria (1972). "vagina dentata". Funk & Wagnalls Standard
    Dictionary of Folklore, Mythology and Legend. entry by Erminie
    W. Voegelin. New York: Funk & Wagnalls.

Mulvey, Laura. "Visual Pleasure and Narrative in Cinema." *Feminist
    Film Theory: A Reader.* Ed. Sue Thornham. NY: NYU Press,
    2006[1999]. 58-69.

Trick r Treat. Dir. Michael Dougherty. Perf. Anna Paquin, Brian Cox
    & Dillon Baker. Warner Bros. 2007

PART TWO: MAGICAL HOMINIDS

Magical Hominids

Of course not every class and not every paper was about bipedal canids, far from it. Examples of these were my zombie and vampire classes, where I couldn't wriggle in werewolves, but could run free with the undead. Yes, they were legit masters level literary classes, taught by the same instructor (I Love you, Dr. Auld). I decided to include vampires, zombies, and magical humans in this book so that I could incorporate the other supernaturals from my educational works (and show you that I really am not a one-trick werewolf, so to speak). Enjoy!

6

BLOOD OF THE SACRED: BLOOD OF THE DAMNED: SANGUINARIANISM IN AMERICA

Names for the following people in this paper have been thrown around more times than curse words at a super bowl. From freak, murderers, Goths, fetishists to ethereal, unknowing and beautiful, the name vampire has been applied to all. The self-actualized vampires are not the cape-clad ravers with fake contacts or lurking serial killers waiting for their next victims, but rather intelligent, well-spoken individuals that simply lack what most of us in the mundane world have…the ability to reproduce the life energy needed for everyday tasks. The true vampire needs to feed off the force of another for focus, euphoria, and most all energy. According to many in the vampire circle, there are three types of vampire, the psychic (psy-feeder), the hybrid (Blood/Psy Feeder) and the sanguine (blood feeder). Each faction, with its unique way of transferring the life essence from one person to another remain the same, people who have been identified as a real vampire. This paper will focus on the sanguine vampire, human people that believe they require the life energy found in human blood to survive.

First and foremost, the distinction of the true vampire from Goths, role-players, fetishists and wannabes must be established. Most of the mundane world views that these are interchangeable and one-in-the-same, however they are quite different. Gothic lifestylers tend to be moody, angst ridden teens with a fascination with death and death iconography. Goths tend to wear black clothes, make-up and hair, and usually adopt some contrasting element to accentuate the darkness (i.e. industrial gothic music, colorful socks, cartoon stuffed animals, etc.). They also very commonly play White Wolf's *Vampire: The Masquerade* to escape into a real world/fantasy life with their friends and like-minded folk. This is the second group, the role-players: not all role-players are Goths and not all Goths are role-players. In some cases, their worlds do overlap, just as other different circles of our life intersect.

There is also another psychological condition within the field of behavioral psychology known as clinical vampirism, or more commonly referred to as Renfield Syndrome, based upon the fictional character of Renfield from Bram Stoker's 1897 novel, *Dracula*. Those that suffer from clinical vampirism, in most cases, are not real vampires either. Renfield Syndrome is described as a pathological and delusional disease, fetishistic and compulsive in nature, where a person (usually a male) experiences a psychological need for blood with a strong sexual component (Sanguinarus). Generally, those that suffer from the syndrome often go through a progression of stages beginning with auto-vampirism (drinking one's own blood) and progressing to vampirism (drinking the blood of others). The compulsion of the vampirism stage may lead a person to committing criminal acts to obtain human blood, such as stealing blood from hospitals and blood banks or going to the extreme of killing someone (Sanguinarus).

There are also vampire lifestylers, which are often involved in vampire communities and can often be mistaken for being real vampires. Vampire lifestylers are people that dress and live a life similar to that of mythical/fictional vampires. They try to emulate the Hollywood and fictional image of a vampire as much as possible:

"Having pale skin from staying out of the sun and/or the use of makeup; Adopting nocturnal lifestyles; wearing fashions seen in movies, television shows, and described in books (most often gothic, Victorian, and/or leather and usually in dark colors); Wearing fake fangs; Wearing WildEyes contact lenses to make their eyes look vampiric (most often, Black-out, Cat Eye, Wildfire, Red Hot and White-out styles); Adopting the use of "old world" language patterns; Decorating their homes to emulate gothic and/or Victorian styles resembling the homes/lairs of vampires seen in movies, television shows and described in books, sometimes including a coffin that they sleep in" (Sphinxcat 1999).

Some will even go to the extent of drinking blood although they have no need to do so. In most cases, vampire lifestylers are regular humans that have chosen to live the lifestyle of a vampire. However, it should be noted that there are also real vampires who choose to live the lifestyle of a vampire (for example, Don Henrie from Sci-Fi Channel's *Mad House*). It is often very easy for real vampires to tell the real vampire lifestylers apart from the human lifestyler (Page 1991:133)

Another group of people that are sometimes involved with the vampire community and mistaken for being real vampires are blood fetishists. Blood fetishists are regular humans who engage in bloodplay (cutting, bloodletting and blood drinking) usually, but not always, within a BDSM setting. Although blood fetishists will often drink blood, they have no need to do so. These are people who receive sexual excitement from blood and its uses. According to real vampires, blood carries the strongest concentration of the energy the need, it is only natural this energy would cause arousal in other areas besides the spirit (Sanguinarius 1997). The fetishists for the most part do not claim to be vampires, but again, their worlds do often cross.

Sanguine vampires (or *sanguinarians*) are vampires who feed by drinking blood. However, it is not the blood itself that they are feeding on. It is the life-force energy contained within the blood. Blood drinking is arguably the most potent form of feeding on life-force energy, and many sanguinarians can thrive for many weeks from a single feeding (A single feeding is often about an ounce or two of blood taken from a willing donor). Sanguinarians often describe blood drinking as a very fulfilling, very powerful and somewhat intoxicating experience. It also tends to be a rather intimate form of feeding (Lady Lilith 2007:23).

The practice that is most readily identified with Vampirism is blood-drinking and bloodletting. A group of members who imbibe blood are referred to as a "feeding circle" and, contrary to media depictions, rarely bite each other on the neck, but usually use razor blades to make cuts into each other's bodies and suck the blood from those cuts. It is important to clarify that not all Vampires engage in this practice. Each group has an official position concerning blood drinking/letting, ranging from a neutral view of simply recognizing that it exists without encouraging it to considering it the highest sacred act of Vampire ritual. All groups post disclaimers concerning the high risk of contracting blood-borne diseases and emphasize that these practices should only occur between consenting adults who have had blood testing and are aware of each other's statuses. Even with official disclaimers, blood drinking/letting is sanctioned, extremely prevalent in the Vampire community, and often engaged in publicly at nightclubs, private havens, and churches.

For Modern Vampires, the use of blood is what separates the dabblers from the Real vampires. In Vampire culture the use of blood is commonly referred to as blood sports, blood play, blood lust, and blood fetishism; it is an expression of sexual, spiritual, recreational, or artistic activities that involve cutting and drinking blood. Blood rituals in the form of sacred acts of worship are fundamental to real Vampire religious beliefs. Blood sports in the form of recreational and/or sexual activities are one of the most dangerous aspects of Vampire culture and are noticeably increasing in popularity. This activity is so popular that there are several websites specifically dedicated to what are called "donors," defined by Vampires as those who give a little of themselves to calm another person's cravings. Donors can be psi (feed on psychic energy) or blood donors and feed on actual blood. Web sites where people can meet and exchange blood include sites like the Blood Letters Donor Community Board.

It is commonly said that real vampires awaken around puberty with the "blood hunger."
A turbulent time for all teens, however, real vampires claim that their hunger for energy becomes the foremost thought on their minds. This is not uncommon in America; teens tend to be lethargic and find they are most active at night and the wish for solitude seems paramount. Clinical psychologists and other health care officials

recognize these symptoms and commonly state that anemia is probably the cause, however vampires never "grow out" of the problem. No number of vitamins or food substitute can bring their energy levels up. It is then that the Goth world appeals to their needs and well as a link to the real-world vampires. The field of behavioral psychology has co-opted the terms psychic vampire and sexual vampire to describe people who have a psychological need for attention and will do whatever they can to get that attention from anyone and everyone, leaving those that interact with them feeling drained (Sanguinarius 1997). In most cases, these people are not real vampires. The drained feeling that people experience when interacting with these people comes from having to tolerate an often uncomfortable and unpleasant situation, but not from an energy feeding.

Like most communities there are rules in which to conduct yourself within the setting. Vampires are no different in that regards. Respect, safety, knowledge and secrecy are paramount in the vampire world. The Rules for the sanguine vampires are simple: "Don't ever feed from animals. Don't bite into your donor unless they agree with it (it's bad to do because of bacteria and bruising). Never take without permission. Never place your mouth on your donor to feed. Unless they agree with it (simply because of bacteria). Don't ever try and save blood to drink it later. Once the blood has left the body it only survives for a few seconds before the energy leaves it and it begins to coagulate" (Sanguinarius 1997).

For the real vampire, keenly aware of health concerns and blood borne pathogens, knowledge about the latest diseases are required reading. Elaborate stages of screening and interviews must take place before donors and vampires actually commit to the bloodletting. Internet websites, such as *Sanguinarius.org* and *Sphinxcatvp.nocturna.org* offer links and invaluable support to new vampire just coming out of the coffin and to those well-established within the community to search for more link minded individuals. Donors are required to submit blood screening tests, inoculations, health reports and some require a psychological exam prior to being admitted into the registered donor sites. The basic safety for the donor and recipient is paramount; the donor must be eighteen years old, at least 110 lbs. and in good health before even being considered for the purpose of donating (Sphinxcat 1999). Once past these health exams, donors are then interviewed with potential recipients: the vampires. Like in a job interview if the parties feel mutually agreed they begin a "courtship", taking all the precautions, most should do when dating an individual before the bloodletting occurs.

The most common misconception about sanguinarians is that they feed by the gallons. They do not, and they make sure their donor knows that. If they were to feed by the pints and gallons they would be sick, for they are human, and their stomachs are not meant to digest blood; they only need a little bit to sustain. Sanguinarians face many problems both physically & mentally. But when you get right down to it, blood is the most important aspect of their condition. A donor is a person who willingly gives a vampire their blood. This may sound simple, but the act of obtaining a donor is probably the hardest things sanguinarians experience. The process of finding a donor can teach us a lot about human nature and friendship (Ramsland 1998:495).

The practice of the blood-letting itself is done in the privacy of the home so that cleanliness is assured. Sterilized instruments such as razor blades, exacto-knives or sharpened dental tools are used to pierce the skin in non-vital locations. There are a few practicing vampires that do use venous blood extraction with a needle and syringe. These people tend to be trained in phlebotomy and similar professions where they would not endanger the donors or themselves. Lancets from diabetic supply store are preferred because they are prepackaged for sterility and for making quick painless, scarless incisions into the skin. Mouth to wound contact is avoided because of bacteria; the blood is simply drained out by syringe or bled into a vial or cup. The blood is consumed immediately, and wound care is given serious attention. Vampire Don Henrie has been quoted as saying that "When he drinks the blood he is so energized that he was bouncing off the walls for days" after the experience (Mid-day Media 2005).

In this article, I have defined what a real vampire is, explained the different types of vampires and their feeding methods and described people often mistaken for real vampires. Vampires do exist; just not in the conventional manner in which we are trained do recognize them. They are human people, not a clique from a nineteen thirties film or novella. There still are many people out there who have other motives. Most of them are teens in their "Vampires are cool!" period, who usually want either a romantic experience or plainly want to be turned they simply do grow out of their vampire faze. However, there are these few who have found their identity outside of the fetish clubs and roleplaying games. They are the real vampires that lead reclusive and secretive lives, not easily willing to give interviews or flaunt their unique place in this world, but just feel accepted. They are the sanguinarians of America.

Works Cited

Lady Lilith, Rev Dr. Vamp Goddess and Lady Nightdancer ELDERS
    COUNCIL
    2007 Welcome to a New Vampire Nation. Haunted Times,
    Volume 2 Issue 2 Spring (23-28)
Midday Media Give me Red. Electronic Document Mid-Day
    Multimedia Ltd. Web. Accessed on April 9, 2007
Modern Goth subculture by Sixwise.com.
    2007 Electronic Document. Web. Accessed April 7, 2007
Page, Carol
    1991 Bloodlust: Conversations with Real Vampires. New
    York, NY. Harper/Collins Press
Reign-Hagen, Mark
    1991 Vampire: The Masquerade. Atlanta: White Wolf
Ramsland, Katherine
    1998 Undercover with Vampires in America Today. New York,
    NY. Harper/Collins Press

---.

    2005 The Human Predator. New York, NY Berkley Publishing
    Group

---.

    2002 The Science of Vampires. New York, NY Berkley
    Publishing Group
Sanguinarius.Org Support for Real Vampires.
    1997 Electronic Document . Web Accessed April 1, 2007
Sphinxcat's Real Vampire Support Page.
    1999 Electronic Document. Web. Accessed March 31, 2007
Thorne, Tony
    1999 Children of the Night: of Vampires and Vampirism.
    London, UK. The Guernsey Press
Trueform Within: Alternative lifestyles.
    2003 Electronic Document. Web. Accessed April 8, 2007
Williamson, Milly
    2005 The Lure of the Vampire: Gender Fiction and Fandom.
    London UK. Wallflower Press.

7

RETURN OF THE VAMPIRE: THE REAVERS OF JOSS WHEDON'S *FIREFLY/SERENITY*

One of the masters of today's contemporary/non-traditional vampire stories is Joss Whedon. He created characters for the series' *Buffy the Vampire Slayer* and *Angel*, who may be vampires, but they are the vampires we want to date, live next door to, and to whom we run in time of need; a far cry from the tales of old where the vampire is a beast of the night, striking horror at the mere mention of the name.

In the short-lived television series *Firefly*, and the subsequent movie *Serenity*, we first heard of Reavers as the unseen boogey-men who committed unspeakable atrocities. The Reavers were to be feared and shunned at all costs, because the mere mention of the name sent war-hardened soldiers into cold sweats. By the time *Serenity* was released, the Reavers embodied the same terror as the vampires of traditional folklore. Utilizing such literary critics as Zanger and Gomez, this paper argues that the Reavers are Joss Whedon's return from the "cute, fluffy puppy with bad teeth" (Spike, *Angel*) to "the Bogey-man from campfire stories" (Jayne, *Firefly*) with the Reavers of *Firefly* and *Serenity*.

The vampires started as nameless, evil entities that walked among humans picking off the weak to feed upon. However, the end of the series' *Buffy the Vampire Slayer* and *Angel* had reduced vampires from fierce predators to innocuous, if not sympathetic, after thoughts. Originally portrayed as traditional vampires, these villainous background characters existed as something to be killed by the Slayer and her friends, but the introduction of vampires who were friends, not foes, changed how the viewer perceived vampires in the two series. Angel and Spike became "the vampire next door", literally and figuratively.

Conversely, Reavers are a group of humans who stalk the fringes of civilized space and have become cannibalistic, monsters that feed off the living flesh of the humans who come into contact with them. The first theory posed within the series is that Reavers are men who traveled to the edge of space and were driven mad by the open nothingness of the universe ("Bushwhacked," *Firefly*). The Reavers remained completely "Othered." To the characters in the series, including their version of a slayer, River Tam, once the line from human to Reaver has been crossed, salvation is no longer an option. The only option considered for the Reavers would simply be extermination.

So why do I argue that they are vampiric? To compare vampires and Reavers we must first look at the distinguishing characteristics of the vampire. In other words what makes a vampire a vampire? Our first thought would probably be that vampires live off the blood of humans. Very basic, but it is a start. The series clearly states that Reavers eat people...alive. They purposely hunt and consume living humans; the series has depicted that, and once a human has died they will not feed upon them. Much like Anne Rice's vampires in the *Vampire Chronicles*, their mythos states that they can never feed off the dead. Unlike Louis and Lestat, however, the Reavers would not suffer any life-threatening problems, should the Reavers consume the dead. They just prefer the living.

Consumption of the blood, as well as, transformation into animals or beasts is also an earmark of vampirism. When Dracula scaled the walls of his castle in a lizard-like way, this marked him, in Jonathan Harkness's mind, as being an unholy terror, but also the faintest hint of primordial man. In this thinking, the Reavers communicate in screams, grunt, and roars. No human diction is portrayed, and although they move bipedally, they move hunched over in quick, primitive gestures. This is classically portrayed Neanderthal man for decades, which is also, primitive man.

With that being said Reavers, like most vampires, were once human beings. Whether the person goes through the change via choice or force; he is no longer the being he once was. According to Whedon in the *Buffy & Angel* series, vampires choose an individual to have as a companion, then through an almost romanticized selection process and deeply personal experience, the "human" is then transformed into a better person, such as the case for Spike, Buffy's arch enemy/comrade/lover. Spike was once known as William, a shy, awkward dork whose heart was stomped on more often than not. When Drusilla, a beautiful yet insane vampire, chose this nerd to be her companion, she unleashed a suave, street smart guy with a Billy Idol look and coolness that a lot of nerds would kill for, no pun intended.

The Reavers on the other hand, were not given a choice. The founding populations of Reavers were turned, chemically, by the Paxilon Hydrochlorate that was added to the air-processors on their home planet of Miranda. The accelerated aggressor responses in the fraction of the population caused normal men to go from ideal, hardworking people to savage creatures that rape, mutilate and consume the remaining population (*Serenity*), a clear case of the switch for Joss from romanticized to repulsed endings for the transformed.

Vampires of tradition, tended to be very like-oriented—Dracula had his brides, Darla had Angel/Angelus, Spike and Drusilla, Lestat had Louis—and in that grand tradition, the Reavers also travel in packs. Though the Reavers are not portrayed as having personal feelings or ties to those who are close to them, they do, however have a need to be a part of a crew. The Reavers fly and live their lives in space. They need to have some working consciousness of the mundane to maintain the vehicles in the sky. The Reavers realize this basic want so that they will survive. Which to expand on that, space is notoriously dark. Like the terran vampires of Earth, the Reavers never stayed on Miranda—nor the other fringe planets they have hit—for anything length of time. The Reavers prefer the vast openness of space to the confining sun-filled planets. Though a sun rays may not be as lethal to the Reavers as it is to other traditional vampires, they spend as little time as possible in its beams.

As the media focus shifted from the plight of the victims to the woes of vampire hero, the proliferation of the female vampire literally exploded. Vampires' according to Gomez, Zanger, and Rice need to be invited into one's life or need the victims consent to be turned by the seductive immortal. These vampires were beautiful, seductive and offering eternal life and who upon being embraced themselves, tended to seek out others to be part of a family base. The Reavers, though, genetically human have been exclusively portrayed as male. Turned by a chemical that, in theory works off the testosterone and aggressive responses, seems to have no effect on females. The Reavers do not seek another familial bond other than to crew their haphazard ships, as the Reavers leave a scene of a recent raid or feeding, the Reavers tend to booby-trap the feeding grounds so that the rescuers or salvagers would then too be consumed by proxy.

The Reavers' methods of embracing their chosen are considered so horrifying that, when faced with capture, their victims almost always attempt suicide, and mercy killings of those who fall into the hands of Reavers are considered humane. The Reavers drive these survivors mad through forcing them to watch the torture of those they were with, effectively turning them into second-hand Reavers. The Reavers also severely mutilate themselves (i.e., by cutting themselves, peeling off their skin, and/or sticking bits of metal into their flesh). At least one normal human during the course of the regular series, a victim of a Reaver attack himself, began exhibiting and emulating Reaver behavior.

In the movie *Serenity*, Reavers are revealed to be humans from the planet Miranda. The Alliance (the government in charge) added a chemical agent known as G-23 *Paxilon Hydrochlorate*, or simply "Pax" (Latin for "peace"), to the planet's air processors. (Serenity. Universal Studios, 2005). This agent was intended to weed out aggressive tendencies in the survivors of the Browncoat rebellion from the Unification War, some twelve years past. These rebels were given a fringe outpost to scratch out a living and to manufacture the "Pax" for future terraforming projects. The Alliance's hurry to push the *Paxilon Hydrochlorate* to subdue the rebel survivors met with tragic consequence. The last thing that the Alliance wanted was to have the subversives start another rebellion, even though the Alliance was successful in quelling the last uprising.

Franco Moretti would call this a classic example of the embodiment of corporate greed, and they are. The Reavers are the product of the Alliance's efforts to quell the Browncoat rebellion and keep the working-class people in their places. The Reavers in turn have consumed and devoured everything the Alliance had planned for Miranda's region of space.

The part of the Reavers themselves can be then seen as the very worst of the consuming youth theorized by Latham. The Reavers' sole purpose is to consume everything and give back nothing. They deplete the resources given them and then like parasites move on to the next host. Unlike the Reavers, the non-traditional vampires of Joss Whedon's universe on several episodes of both series, tried to utilize their resources and use humans sparingly, to set up industry as to not deplete their food sources. Reavers devour until there is nothing left, save the lone survivor that then joins their ranks. They are not interested in long-term dividends: Just to destroy.

Joss Whedon began his journey with vampires be a means to an end, an antagonist for his slayer. Slowly these vampires wormed there way into the realm of friend hero and lover some even with souls; an ultimate in the coolest of the cool immortal being, that everyone wanted to be/with. With *Firefly*, Whedon ushered in the return of the creature that swoops down from the night and eats your flesh while you watch. A being that once struck terror in the hearts and minds of Victorian Europe, the vampire has been reintroduced as the space dwelling and aggressively soulless Reaver.

Works Cited

"Bushwhacked." Perfs. Nathan Fillion, Gina Torres. Firefly. DVD. FOX, 2003.

Chambers, Jamie. Serenity Roleplaying Game. Lake Geneva, WI: Margaret Weis, 2005.

DeCandido, Keith R.R. Serenity. New York: Pocket Star, 2005.

Firefly: The Official Companion, Volume One. London, England: Titan, 2006.

Gomez, Jewelle. "Recasting the Mythology: Writing Vampire Fiction." Blood Read. Philadelphia: U of PA Press, 1997. 85-92.

Hollinger, Veronica. "Fantasies of Absence: The Postmodern Vampire." Blood Read. Philadelphia: U of PA Press, 1997. 199-212.

Latham, Rob. "Consuming Youth: The Lost Boys Cruise Mallworld." Blood Read. Philadelphia: U of PA Press, 1997. 129-147.

Moretti, Franco. "A Capital Dracula." Dracula: A Norton Critical Edition. Bram Stoker. Eds. Nina Auerbach and David J. Skal. New York: Norton, 1997. 431-444.

Ramsland, Katherine, Ph.D. The Science of Vampires. New York: Berkley, 2002.

"Serenity." Perfs Nathan Fillion, Gina Torres. Firefly. DVD. FOX, 2003.

Serenity. Dir. Joss Whedon. Perfs. Nathan Fillion, Chiwetel Ejiofor. Film. Universal Studios, 2005.

Whedon, Joss. Serenity: The Official Visual Companion. London, England: Titan, 2005.

Zanger, Jules. "Metaphor into Metonymy: The Vampire Next Door." Blood Read. Philadelphia: U of PA Press, 1997. 17-26.

Zynda, Lyle. "We're All Just Floating in Space." Finding Serenity: Anti-Heroes, Lost Shepherds and Space Hookers in Joss Whedon's Firefly. Ed. Jane Espenson. BenBella, 2004. 85-96.

8

WOMEN, WITCHCRAFT AND SOCIETY: UNDERSTANDING HOW THE TERM "WITCH" IS USED TO CONTROL WOMEN PAST AND PRESENT

"Burn the Witch!" "Witch-Hunt!" "Witch!" These are all terms of pending violence, rage, fear and accusations of flirting with darkness that threatens the society in which we live. "Witch" is a term often slung at social outcasts who possess a mysterious knowledge or particular talent that, for whatever reason, places pressure upon the status quo. This term has come out on top of the near vulgar, but acceptable way in which to accuse, demoralize and ostracize people. Why is that? What power does the word "Witch" have that it causes some civilized people to rally into anger so quickly? For whatever reason accusing a Christian woman of being a witch, even in today's high tech American society, can bring that woman to fighting rage, depression and fear. The power of the word, still has a mysterious hold, although now lessened to some extent with new media depictions of the sexy nubile witch, it still has a deep seeded hold upon people and their perceived meaning of Witch.

Medieval Europe has often been written about in context of witch trials, where some innocent and some not-so-innocent people were put to death because of their perceived crimes against God and the Church. Often women were the targets of malicious witch-hunts in which they were stripped of their dignity, families and often their lives. The role of women in the witch craze phenomenon takes on various levels of meaning as one delves into the cases by region, religion, time and circumstances. Although times have changed, and women have achieved much within societies, the modern American woman and Pagan are still frequently referred to as witches. I find this concept intriguing and so I have decided to delve further into the meaning of the terms "Woman" and "Witch" placing these ideas into historical contexts of "Past" and "Present." As such, this paper will analyze not only the placement of women within the culture, religion and society of Medieval Europe, but also how the notions of the past are still reflected upon women and Pagans of today in America, where the term "Witch" is used as a controlling factor for women.

The term 'Witch-hunt' itself, has become a generic term, referring to any situation in which a 'guilty party' is, essentially, tried and convicted in absentia, without any 'firm' evidence—indeed, in a typical witch-hunt, guilt is presumed from the outset, and the focus of the hunt becomes getting the accused to admit her guilt. Often, these so-called 'confessions' are brought about by way of verbal trickery, or by questioning the loyalty or past conduct of the accused. This method, in which the term 'Witch' is used to control an individual, has been utilized since the middle ages.

Medieval Society

To properly analyze the role of gender and women, we first must look at Western society overall and examine the expected roles for women and the actual roles over time, beginning with the Middle Ages (approximately ~1000 through 1600 C.E.). Medieval Europe was a under the rule of patriarchal governments and Catholic church doctrine; however, multiple wars, various diseases and plagues had taken their toll on the overall population of Europe, so strict guidelines of the societies had to be flexible enough to allow some overlapping of women's and men's traditional duties (Hester et al 293). Women often had to farm and take care of animals, rather than just perform household duties, especially if her husband was away at war or had been killed by pestilence. Women of that time were expected to know how to run the household, inside and out, and had to maintain the family's integrity under adversity. It seemed as if women often took on characteristically male roles for the good of the household and community.

One concept, however, was strictly enforced: order within the community. Any deviation that was considered "over the line", such as cross-dressing, homosexuality in men and female education other than seminary training, was punishable by land forfeiture, striped titles and possibly death. Therefore, it was not only women who suffered from societal sanctions, but also the men. However, it was with the Malleus *Maleficarum*, a famous witch-hunting manual used by both Catholics and Protestants, written in 1486 by Heinrich Kramer and Jacob Sprenger, outlines how to identify a witch, what makes a one more likely to be a witch, how to put a witch to trial and how to punish a witch. The book defines a witch as evil and typically female. It had tremendous influence in the witch trials in England and on the European continent, as well as influence on American soil. "The Malleus was used as a judicial case-book for the detection and persecution of witches, specifying rules of evidence and the canonical procedures by which suspected witches were tortured and put to death. Thousands of people (primarily women) were judicially murdered because of the procedures described in this book, for no reason than a strange birthmark, living alone, mental illness, cultivation of medicinal herbs, or simply because they were falsely accused (often for financial gain by the accuser). The Malleus serves as a horrible warning about what happens when intolerance takes over a society. And similar tracts that the focus became more about the unholy woman tempting the virtuous man." (Hare)

This paragraph's closing simplifies the explanation of the attitudes towards women of the 14th century. The Malleus did not solely target women as witches, but it did warn men of their lower standing, emotion and ethics as compared to the virtuous man.

Medical Field

From the Middle Ages forward, medical treatments by physicians were strictly a male purview, but midwifery was securely in the realm of "women's work." Any treatment of birth control, conception and menstruation was performed by the local midwife. Popular culture had Americans believing that it was the medical profession that was the driving force in the witch crazes in order to drive out midwifery (Ehrenreich and English 15), but in fact the medical profession viewed midwives as necessary. Men never entered a birthing chamber, because to do so was punishable by death. Should a woman take up a man's trade such as blacksmith, she was immediately shied away from and shunned in the community and was a suspect for anything out of the ordinary such as a neighbor's cow giving sour milk, odd weather patterns or failures in crops. Cunning folk, especially women, with their trade in herbal remedies often became targets, as they seemed to possess unnatural, but effective cures to many ailments of a diseased and malnourished population. The cunning women would then take on a daughter or another female as apprentice to ensure the knowledge not be lost. As populations grew, this was the only way, along with midwifery, that a single woman could sustain a living. If she was not a midwife or if she did not have the means to enter a convent, she then became a burden upon her community and had to rely on charity. However, in times of famine and drought, charity dried up and compassion turned to guilt, which led to stress in the community. The stress built up until it exploded from a catalyst linked back to the "crazy cat lady" in some way so that social bonds are reformed, and a communal order is restored. Unfortunately, the relief was generally at the cost of another life. These stresses were localized at percolated from the bottom of the social ladder up. Rarely did royal decree cause a witch craze; it did the opposite by suppressing them.

"Good Wife, Good Mother"

The idea of the "Good Wife, Good Mother" was the highest social rank a woman could achieve. Politics within the female hierarchy in a community was fierce. Mobility within that structure was the only power women could wield. When a female child was born, her sole purpose was that to become a fruitful wife, hard working to please her husband and bearing the children of the head of household. She would work her way through the social ranks within the women of the community until she achieved this goal. Women who did not fit this mold, either by death of her spouse, or because she was post-menopausal, a spinster, a closet lesbianism or simply older, she would be suspect for being a witch, as her social status among the other women was already lowered, making her an easy target.

These women would no longer be considered a productive member of society. This created tension between women in families and households, as when a child is now higher statused in the community than her mother or grandmother. Illegitimate children and unwed pregnant women were not given any assistance. These women were considered amoral and were shunned; often they would work as midwives and were most likely to be accused by other women of witchcraft. Jealousy, envy, and revenge would be a women's only sense of power she had in the world at this time.

Childbirth

Childbirth was considered "woman's work" that did not require assistance by a trained male physician; however, complications could and often did occur. If a woman should die in childbirth, it would not be uncommon for the husband to remarry a younger woman to maintain the children and home. Family tensions between the children from a husband's previous marriage and the new wife would lead to resistance of the new arrangement any way they know how to; for example, accusing the new mother of witchcraft, just as the case of Judith Wagner. Family tensions also took on other guises as well, such as the case of Anne Gunther. After exhibiting classic symptoms of possession, she accused family rivals of witchcraft. This case however, through pressure from her father, was forced to perform the "possession" in order for him to deal with local land rivals. This case was brought before the king were Anne confessed her father's wrong doing and lead a normal life away from him. The people that Anne accused were acquitted, and her father was given a fine (Sharpe).

Jealousy of the laying-in maid was also a factor in the accusation of witchcraft. A pregnant wife is unable to fulfill her wifely duties and a laying-in maid would be brought in to oversee the household until after the new baby was born. Often times the laying-in maid was an experienced mother or spinster who no longer had duties at home and needed money. Generally, they would be older and would often be accused of witchcraft if the baby was born with a defect or if the husband and children got too close or in the worst-case scenario the baby died. It was the suspicious outsider, the laying-in maid, that was often targeted. If the laying-in maid was older than the young wife, she and the husband would have more in common and speak as peers as the husband took on a fatherly role with his young bride, rather than partner.

The possible camaraderie between the older man and woman could insight the wife into accusation of witchcraft. If a wealthy family used a wet nurse, the baby would then be lacking the colostrum needed for a strong immune system. Many times, the infant would be fussy with the mother, colicky or even die. This placed the wet nurse in a place of suspicion even with the most impeccable references because she was the only one who had contact with the baby.

The Church (Virgin/Whore Dichotomy)

In regard to the church, the witch-craze was a phenomenon that predominantly targeted women who did not fall into the "orthodox" view of the theological image of woman. Which was an impossible ideal, for the Virgin Mary was considered the ideal woman. Chaste, pure and free of temptation, she was not sexualized in any way nor would she lure men from their vow of purity from God. Men who exited the seminaries after years of confinement during their educations were suddenly confronted with the reality of what women are. This frightened and angered some to the point of retaliation as with such tracts as the Malleus Maleficarum which depicted women as weak and easily corrupted, temptations to be subdued and punished lest they lead good men astray. Their effects on these men were everything that the Virgin Mary was not, which only "proved" their allegiance with the devil and emphasized that all women who were not protected virgins were "naturally" creatures that needed to be tamed, sheltered and suppressed.

It is often believed that during the Renaissance Period of Europe (starting in the late 15th century C.E.), that pressure from the church sent untold hundreds if not thousands of men, women and children to their deaths as a result of accusations of witchcraft. Alas, this simply is not the case, according to records from court proceedings of that time; it was often a result from a trend known as "pressure from beneath" (Sharpe 33). It was largely, but not always, a case in which members of the community who were at odds for whatever reason failed to reach a satisfactory answer to their problems from local governments and turned to the Catholic Church for guidance.

When a witch or werewolf was singled out in the community, a strange phenomenon occurred: social unification of a previously disjointed group. Solidarity lent comfort to the township and kinship where there may have been strife, well maybe not for the accused, but rather for the community at large. When this phenomenon occurred, it is found that the church was actually a calming force that ebbed a tide of panic that could have easily swept through a township, killing many more than what already was. As contrary as that sounds, the idea is simple in that it always comes back to control of the populace. You see, for close to 700 years, from the Middle Ages to the Renaissance to the Enlightenment Period, the populations of Europe (and by extension, the small colonial nations in the New World) were in constant turmoil. The Crusades, territorial warfare, starvation and plagues left the collective psyche of the people scared, fractured and fatalistic. The fragmenting of the church following the Protestant Reformation in the 15th century C.E. also left people confused and uncertain. As governments stabilized and the Witch Reformations of 1663, in which the overall view of these cases as consuming too much of the state's money and intellectual time, the reported accusations and subsequent trials for the witches began to decrease (Sharpe 73). Accusations of witchcraft fell by the wayside in the wake of Enlightenment ideals that stressed science and the mind over superstition and religious controls. If indeed there were still witches in Europe and America during 19th and early 20th centuries, they were hidden well in their broom closets.

Everything Old is New Again

In 1921, Margaret Murray, a modern anthropologist and noted Egyptologist wrote a book called The Witch-cults in Western Europe, which began the rebirth of Paganism in England that quickly crossed the pond into the United States as the spiritualist movement of the late 1800's and early 1900's swept the nation. New "born-again pagans" adopted the teachings Gerald Gardner and the Murray's book weaving into Wicca, an Earth based spiritual religion loosely based on a mixture of druidism, shamanism and a dash of old fashion herbology. The ingredients worked well for an American country that was wracked with war, depression and a geographical disconnect from head of the powerful European Churches. Pagan holidays were also given new life with the advent of the greeting card and gift industry so holidays like Halloween began anew.

Halloween Witch

Halloween is one of the four highest holidays of the pagan celebrations and is often considered the greatest of the four, sometimes called the Great Sabbath. The Great Sabbath is when the "Halloween witch" takes the time to observe the supernatural powers of this world and other worlds and ponder the mysteries that lie in both. It is a night for honoring ancestors, celebrating the harvest, and ringing in the New Year (which begins on November 1st), but it was images of the "Crone" or "Old Hag" that grew to become one of the most endearing and long-lasting Halloween images we as Americans have...the Witch. (Morgan, 38)

Every October the History Channel or Travel Channel televises some documentary or film of the "Burning Times" and how the Witch Trials of Medieval Europe was the birthplace of the Witch and its evolution into either the green-skinned witch from Oz or three nubile young witch sisters are their direct descendants. Although now the media is quick to show new stories of "sky-clad" rituals of modern Wicca practitioners, properly pixilated out for their modest viewing audience. While stating keen interest in observing their religious practices, the outcome was merely a ruse in allowing good Christians a voyeuristic and safe position of judgment.

New Age Religion

Gerald B. Gardner, a retired British civil servant, is known as the "Grandfather" of almost all Neo-Wicca. He was initiated into a, English coven in 1939 and persuaded them to let him write a book about Wicca, which was subsequently released in the form of a novel called *High Magic's Aid* (1949). He then wrote *Witchcraft Today* (1954) in which he described additional details about the faith. Largely promulgated and popularized in the 1950s, these books are considered the most influential of the Traditions among the Neo-Pagan community. Gardnerian Wicca is both traditional and family with principles of love and trust. It is a structured religion with definite hierarchy within each coven (a matriarchy exists with the High Priestess being the leader). The typical

Gardnerian view of the Goddess is that of a dominant Three-Faced Goddess (Maid, Mother, and Crone) with a Male Consort. Gardnerian Wicca requires ritual nudity and Norse Wicca is based out of it. Gerald Gardner was a member of the Ancient Druid Order and, along with Ross Nichols, founded the Order of Bards, Ovates, and Druids (Stuart, 26; Russell, 164). More often than not, these newly found free spirited "Wiccans" were not viewed as threatening or harmful, and the term "witch" became for a short time a romanticized folly, but not a religion.

Modern Interpretation of the Witch

When the flower child movement of the 1960's began, the draw of the Nature based religions to the flower children seemed natural and expected. The Vietnam War, civil rights movement and many other social changes began to wear on the collective psyche of the nation. The polarization of the American populace began again with a strong draw to be "A Good Christian" or "A Devil Worshipping Witch." Sinister implications began to arise concerning the media's depiction of witches. Gone are the good time romps of Samantha and Darren, to the dark and ominous "villain of the week" character.

This was poignantly marked after the August 1969 murders committed by the Manson family in Los Angeles. The age of the innocent Witch and flower child were over, thrusting the term "witch" back into the negative limelight with a new vengeance. Bewitched and I dream of Jeanie were replaced with television shows that did not promote the supernatural life style of witches or others in a positive light, but rather aired television shows with good wholesome characters fighting the "witches." Additionally, the Federal Communication Commission began a drive to censor the language used in prime time (8-10pm) television, and the term "witch" replaced "bitch" subtly by many program writers to bypass the vulgarity restrictions. Although the term was not being used to subjugate women, per say, it was being used to control or manipulate existing rules and boundaries.

The Work Place/Motherhood and Home

Since 1920, women have had the right to vote. Since the sixties, we have had reproductive choices other than marriage, convent or death. Careers for women have now reached further than the wildest dreams of their medieval sisters. In contemporary American culture, it is becoming commonplace for women to reach high-level positions in governments, churches, businesses and families, so why is it that when a woman dares reach for the highest level…she is called "Witch"? Perhaps the answer can be found in a deep seeded gesture from back to the days when the church and state were one and the same, and it was the easiest way to call into question the purity of a woman or belittle her intentions.

What else is woman but a foe to friendship, an inescapable punishment, a necessary evil, a natural temptation, a desirable calamity, domestic danger, a delectable detriment, an evil nature, painted with fair colours [sic]…Women are by nature instruments of Satan -- they are by nature carnal, a structural defect rooted in the original creation" (Malleus Maleficarum 1485).

The Influence of the Church Today / Radical Christian Backlash

Modern Church influence over popular culture, media and political institutions have had a unique and profound effect on the treatment of women since women won the right to vote in 1920. Christian based churches began to loosen the grip on the role of women within the church.

Ministry positions allowed the faithful and devout woman a place within the rigid hierarchy of the traditional "all boys" club where they can both be in a position of power and serve God.

One would comfortably affirm that the United States is currently going through a period of economic unrest and upheaval. As such, it is common that people as a whole revert to a radical mindset when faced with troubling times. The upswing of church memberships after the 9/11 disaster, gave what appeared to be a renewed sense of faith. People (generalized) sought comfort from a fear they had no control over and for the most part never heard of. Until the attacks, few people off the street knew who or what Al Qaida was, now that name is forever linked to 9/11 and everyone (generalized) knows the meaning. This again is also an example of solidarity via the "othering" of Islamic peoples… "We aren't Muslim, we are Christian."

The level of discomfort brought about by the attacks, slowly simmer within the religious environment and boil into separatist factions of Christian churches who use the bible as weapons and platforms for hate and violence against more than just the Arab speaking world, but also towards homosexuals, soldiers return from the war in Iraq or anyone unfortunate enough to cross their path that day. All too often, the first word slung at this newly found "other" is generally "witch."

Modern Witch Hunts

Religious terrorism is intimately connected to current forces of geopolitics. Although most cases of religious separatism do not involve violence, there are cases in which harassment, vandalism and even murder are carried out in the name of "The Church." The terms "Devil Worshiper" and "Witch" are the first cast at a target. Once the terrorist groups make threats, usually, other factions follow suit in harassing people to change their businesses, lifestyle or even move from the community. Lending to the theory that "The Church" is a silent but power controller of regional communities. According to Mark Juergensmeyer, this religious terrorism consists of acts that terrify by the party committing the act; accompanied by religious motivation, justification, organization, or worldview. Religion although in itself is not a "bad institution"; it is just that sometimes it is used in combination with other factors, and sometimes as the primary motivation to control the masses.

Bruce Hoffman has characterized modern religious terrorism as having three traits:

- The perpetrators must use religious scriptures to justify or explain their violent acts or to gain recruits
- Clerical figures must be involved in leadership roles
- Apocalyptic images of destruction are seen by the perpetrators as a necessity [4]

This example is carried out on a widespread small scale with the recent "witch" children of Nigeria in West Africa as well as Papua New Guinea. With women being primary targets, these cases take a more sinister turn in Nigeria in West Africa, where the persecutions focus on children. Despite the distance between the Papuan and the West African cultures, the scenario is similar: the so-called witches are blamed for some misfortune within the community or held responsible for social ills. Like days of old, sometimes they are considered witches simply because their behavior is unruly or socially unacceptable.

The 'witches' are singled out usually by men within the communities that wield spiritual power over the people: Christian pastors in Nigeria, or elder, male, tribal council members in Papua. The sentence is banishment, torture or death. In Nigeria, it is usually parents or community 'vigilantes' that enact the penalties, while in Papua there are organized groups of 'witch hunters' whose only purpose is to mete out the punishment. Either way the situation is still the same: control the people, control their money.

One interpretation from observation is that both cultures mentioned are under incredible pressure from unstable governing forces, especially Nigeria, where there is radical and fierce competition for religious beliefs. Although this Region in West Africa is not unique, but shared, the fact of why this particular region crossed the human ethical line for the sake of money is not clearly known. These factors mentioned were also prevalent in the Middle Ages in Europe at the time of the witch-hunts there. This further lends credence to the theory that larger social stresses tend to have larger amounts of "witch occurrences" than times of peace. The uncertainty of life leads people to try to control the world around them and thus become hyper-aware of subtle differences from the perceived norm.

Like when an earthquake hits, the earthen unrest is out of your immediate control and as an unconscious reaction to try and stop falling household items kicks in, sometimes to the point of breaking items one would normally would try to save but like a television set that you fear will fall on your child so you throw it to the ground to prevent that from happening. Logic is cast aside when your world is unstable, whether it be earth or governing body and scared individuals do drastic things in times of crisis. Fear, superstition and greed have gripped these communities and Americans at times believe this would never happen here…again, which this is not the case, although not carried to the extreme as Papua or Nigeria, incidents of violence, bigotry or discrimination have occurred in the good ol' US of A…recently. Countless incidents of businesses within small communities that feature New Age books, holistic healing or alternative lifestyles were shunned, vandalized and refused business licenses based on "Christian" beliefs. The governing body clearly has "The Church" in seats of power…again.

Conclusion

In conclusion, although women held little power in the realm of church and state in medieval Europe, they did have a strict hierarchal subculture between them in the community. This power ebbed and flowed as the women grew, became wives and mothers and eventually becoming social outcasts is one form or another. These power and status changes were often linked with witchcraft or the accusations there of. The influence of the educated brought a double-edged sword to women of this time period in that men who were educated in seminary school sought an unrealistic ideal of a woman and lashed out against them, such as with the Malleus Maleficarum. The woman was a strangely seductive and easily corruptible creature to the men freshly released from the seclusion of seminary school. Coupled with the social pressures from the community and state, many women fell in line for an accusation of witchcraft. Just as today when women of power, alternate lifestyle or independent spirit fall under the same scrutiny, retaliatory actions are made. The term "Witch" is often slung about, but rarely are the women burned at the stake anymore.

Works Cited

Akrong, Abraham. "Neo-Witchcraft Mentality in Popular Christianity." Research Review 16.1 (2000) 1-12.

Anderson, Allen and Raymond Gordon. "Witchcraft and the Status of Women-The case of England." The British Journal of Sociology. 29.2 (1978):171-184.

Barstow, Anne Llewellyn. "On Studying Witchcraft as Women's History: A historiography of the European witch persecutions." Journal of   Feminist Studies and Religion. 4.2 (1988):7-19.

Bever, Edward. "Witchcraft, female aggression, and power in the early modern community." Journal of Social History. 35.4 (2002):955-988.

Brain, James. "An Anthropological Perspective on the Witchcraze." Magic, Witchcraft, and Religion: A Reader in the Anthropology of Religion. Ed. Pamela A. Moro and James E. Myers. New York: McGraw-Hill 2010. 283-290.

Cockrell, Amanda. "Harry Potter and the Witch Hunters: A Social Context for the Attacks on 'Harry Potter'." Journal of American Culture 29.1 (2003) 24-30.

Dunwich, Gerina. The Pagan Book of Halloween. New York: Penguin Compass 2000.

Ehrenreich, Barbara and Deirdre English. Witches, Midwives, and Nurses: A History of Women Healers. New York: The Feminist Press, 1973.

Hare, John Bruno. Internet Sacred Text Archive. Internet Sacred Text Archive. 2008. Web. 29 Nov. 2009.

Hester, Marianne, et al. Witchcraft in Early Modern Europe: Studies in Culture and Belief. Melbourne, Australia: Cambridge UP, 1996.

Kaminer, Wendy. "American Gothic." American Prospect 11.26 (2000) 38-39.

Kramer, Heinrich and James Sprenger. The Malleus Maleficarum. Mineola, NY: Dover, 2009.

Maxwell-Stuart, P.G. Witchcraft in Europe and the Modern World, 1400- 1800. New York: Palgrave, 2001.

Morgan, Sheena. The Real Halloween: Ritual and Magic for Kids and Adults. New York: Barrons, 2002.

Moura, Ann. Origins of Modern Witchcraft. St. Paul, MN: Llewellyn. 2000.

Peach, Lucinda Joy. Women and World Religions. Upper Saddle River NJ: Prentice Hall. 2002.

Phillips, Jan. "The Craft of the Wise." Ms Jan. 1993: 78.

Rowlands, Alison. Witchcraft and Old Women in Early Modern Germany." Past & Present. 173 (2001) 50-89.

Rublack, Ulinka. The Crimes of Women in Early Modern Germany. Oxford: Clarendon. 1999.

Russell, Jeffrey B. & Brooks Alexander. A History of Witchcraft: Sorcerers, Heretics & Pagans 2nd Ed. New York: Thames & Hudson. 2007.

Sharpe, James. The Bewitching of Anne Gunter. New York NY: Rutledge Press, 1999.

Shufelt, Catherine Armetta. "Something Wicked This Way Comes": Constructing the Witch in Contemporary American Popular Culture. Diss. Bowling Green State University, 2007. Bowling Green, OH.

Stuart, P.G. Maxwell. Witchcraft: A History. Brimscombe Port: Tempus Publishing. 2004.

9

"ARE YOU MY MUMMY?": ATTAINING LIFE THROUGH BIRTH FROM THE UNDEAD PARENT

The notion of motherhood is generally described a blessed event, an unparalleled experience in which the combination of two people creates a new being in their image to continue the miracle of life…continue clichés blah blah blah. The reality is that birth is a violent, bloody assault to your body, mind and soul. The physical reality is that a woman's body is forever changed by the act of birth; her hips are widened, her breasts hang heavy and her skin, although glowing before, now bares stretch marks and darkened patches. Her psyche also changes: her focus becomes split between the living and unborn, these changes overtake her at times, without her being aware of them. Ultimately, however, this darkness before the dawn is played out with the arrival of the new baby, a shiny new soul that gives hope to those who experience or witness the event…just like a zombie apocalypse.

This paper will argue that, with the introduction of a zombie apocalypse, the undead themselves become the metaphorical "birth mothers" to new and shiny people experiencing life for possibly the first time in their lives and that their former lives are the mirror of their previously living assailants or as they will be called "Zombie Mums." This paper will utilize the application of critics William Larkin, Hamish Thompson, Matthew Walker, and Dale Jacquette to explore how, through the introduction of zombies into the lives of two separate film characters, their lives are changed by violence and blood. It explores how ultimately, their birthing into a shiny new person, gives hope to us (the viewer) and hope for their future…living in a zombie apocalypse.

In Hamish Thompson's article "She's Not Your Mother Anymore, She's a Zombie", Thompson argues that psychological continuity in zombies permits moral devaluation of zombies and thus their personal identity is compromised allowing we the survivors a moral ground to destroy the monstrous body (28). With their identities forever gone the only thing left to do is put down the body, permanently killing the host by decapitation or immolation. This interpretation dealing with the continuity of body, mind and soul plays out in both Helen Robinson from the Lionsgate Film *Fido* (2006) and Shaun from Universal Studios' film *Shaun of the Dead* (2004). This concept also walks hand-in-hand with William Larkin's article entitled "Res Corporealis: Persons, Bodies and Zombies" in which Larkin argues that the physical continuity over the psychological identity allows us, the survivors to destroy the zombies (15). The presence of missing limbs, flesh and whatnot creates feelings of abjection (Cole 189) and disconnection, permitting us to rectify a wrong by putting the obviously "flawed" zombie back into the ground or place of origin.

Matthew Walker's article "When There's No More Room in Hell, The Dead will shop the Earth: Romero and Aristotle on Zombies and Consumption" argues the idea of Pleonexia: the desire of desire, a self-perpetuating cycle of always needing to have the next, better thing or just plain surviving with no actual forward progression (81). He also discusses the idea of Eudaimonia: the state of ultimate happiness, which is the culmination of achieving the desires of Pleonexia (81). This concept is critical to the exposition of the birthing process of both Helen Robinson and Shaun from the films, as it reveals their emergence into a new world with new hope, just as a newborn infant blinks at the light of day after passing through the birth canal.

Finally, "Zombie Gladiators" by Dale Jacquette, argues the subtle differences of Automata: the automaton and the Conscios: the real person (105). The philosophical zombie (or automation) is only recognizable by a small mark on the back of the neck, but is otherwise indistinguishable from humans. Each performs identically and appears to have an identity, yet only conscios actually HAVE identity, while the automata merely perform it, giving the conscios license to deal with them as seen fit. This concept will apply in analyzing Helen and Shaun prior to their "coming out" or "births."

The character of Helen Robinson from the film *Fido*, is pregnant and, living with a case of Pleonexia in these suburban automata of a human life. Helen is married to Bill, a well-off man, and they have one son, Timmy, who is intelligent and soulful. The Robinsons live in an idealistic suburban setting with a house, white picket fence, garden parties, and a "dog," a perceived perfect, safe life. However, Helen is not happy. She often tries to engage the family in conversation that challenges the expectation of "proper behavior" as valued by her husband, a contraction to her womb-like existence. Helen wants to discuss zombie ownership, as well as the potential of becoming a zombie after death, while her husband is terrified of zombies and ultimately wishes to be buried with a "head casket", ensuring he will not rise again as undead. He does not wish to be "reborn" in any sense, and he is in many ways, dead already.

Helen's sole focus is on having what others have and cultivating the appearance of being perfect regardless of the feelings of her family and herself. For example, when Timmy comes home having been beaten up by bullies, she is more concerned about the reaction of the neighbors than on the health and welfare of her child. Timmy feels isolated from a seemingly inhuman mother. She is colder and less interested in him than a zombie would be, and when the family acquires a zombie servant, it is significant that Timmy names him "Fido" (Latin for "I trust"): he trusts Fido more than he trusts his distant family. To Timmy, Helen is an automaton, devoid of feeling and consciousness.

The state of surviving without end is a loop of desire that cannot be achieved according to Walker's argument because it is to desire immortality to be *athanatos* or deathless (85). Helen continues to exist in a state of automata, until she brings home Fido, the family's first zombie. For the first time Helen is given attention from someone other than her husband. Fido, and, consequently Timmy, give her love and respect from within the family and this leads to respect from others outside the family. The neighbors who share garden parties and clearly denote zombie-ownership as a necessary status symbol, reject Helen when she does not have a zombie. Her acquisition of Fido not only provides her with equality within the neighborhood, but Fido's devotion to her gives her a sense of safety and well-being.

When Fido's control collar is broken, Fido attacks and kills a foul neighbor woman who constantly belittles Timmy and lays judgment upon Helen. Helen begins to feel sympathy for Fido, when she dresses him in one of her husband's seldom worn suits for a funeral that Bill obsessively yearns for as his life is consumed by the notion of death. When Helen tells him that she is expecting a baby, his response is to see the money required for the funeral, not the hope of the future. This too is an example of Walker's idea of Pleonexia, as Bill only lives for death a never-ending existence of survival that does not nurture life but extinguishes it. Bill's psyche is that of automata, doing things automatically without consciousness, which if we follow Jacquette's idea means Bill is the zombie, marked only by his actions. He is merely "acting" or "performing" his life and not really a *conscio*, like Helen. Conversely, Fido acts with compassionately when he saves Timmy from the bullies, and when he comforts Helen from her loneliness…It can then be argued that unlike Bill, Fido is the *conscio*, acting from true feelings, even though he is marked as a zombie. However, it is Helen's emergence into life that occurs when Fido begins filling her new soul with hope, promise for the future and love. Helen's painful actual "birth" is the death of her husband Bill, the automata man who kept her life tethered by an umbilicus of perceived normality that kept her safe but unhappy and longing for freedom.

The pain of Bill's death by the hands of Zom-Com's head of security ushers in a new life for Helen as she is not given the time to grieve, but is forced to survive and save Timmy, as well as Fido, from the zombie mayhem and violence. The fear, adrenaline and copious amounts of blood and panic is the "birthing room" to Helen as she is delivered to safety with her son, new baby and lover into her suburban home and safety. Love, life and eudemonia are found when Fido (a zombie and her ultimate parent/partner) comes into her life and delivers her from her sterile "safe" womb with a view and into the life of in which she truly did want…happiness and love

The character of Shaun in the film *Shaun of the Dead*, is not pregnant, but living a child-like, automata life. When the zombie outbreak occurs, Shaun begins his birthing process through blood ("you got red on you"), pain (the loss of his human mother, Barbara) and ultimate happiness (with Liz, his girlfriend), when his buddy Ed (as a new zombie mother) gives Shaun the gift of his life with the girl he loves. Shaun walks through his day stuck in a circle of perpetual survival with no upward mobility or room for advancement, He goes through the same dull routine every day and when the word around him drastically changes, he does not notice. As he sits on the bus, as he talks to his employees, every aspect of his life is "just enough." What marks him as a philosophical zombie is his nametag – everyone who appears to be an *automata* in this film wears a name badge showing their status in society as "customer service workers" or mediocre. The first zombie that Shaun meets face to face is "Mary." He knows this because of her plastic nametag. It is significant that her name is "Mary", as that name is considered to be a "boring, mediocre name", and as a zombie, Mary is not much different from the bored, checkout girl we glimpsed at the beginning of the film. Her facial expressions are the same and when Shaun and Ed first encounter her, they believe her to be drunk. Shaun's failure to see the zombie apocalypse is significant because metaphorically, he is already a zombie and he cannot see them as outsiders. He is one of them already, and it is difficult to see something from within. He cannot see that his routine, boring life is not much different from the shuffling undead.

Shaun is an electronic store's assistant manager who barely scrapes together his life long enough to go to the Winchester Pub every night. His girlfriend dumps him, he is on the outs with his step-father, and his best friend holds him back in almost every aspect of his life...Shaun is living in what Matthew Walker writes "as a state of Pleonexia" the state of merely surviving in a perpetual cycle never achieving anything (85). He walks through his day and life in an automated state every morning and evening never noticing the zombie apocalypse that has landed squarely in his flat.

At the beginning of the film, Shaun is res *corporealis*: he is physically taking up space, but nothing more (Larkin 16). He is not a thinking creature because he does not have to be – he is attached by at least four umbilical cords to his Barbara/Mum, Pete, Ed and Liz. Barbara has never allowed Shaun to grow up: he will always be "Pickle", and he is always talked down to by her. She has no expectations from him, she sees him as the seven-year-old he was when his father died, and stepfather Philip entered their lives. Pete, who has a good job and owns the home Shaun lives in reflects what Shaun could be if he put forth any effort; if Shaun applied himself and stopped allowing Ed and his own life to hold him back. Pete represents what Shaun could be if he discarded the chains of the automata and began living as a *conscio*. Ed is the friend from childhood that we all have and cannot seem to get off the couch no matter where you move. He ties Shaun to his past and prevents him from having a future. Nevertheless, Ed is not a villain: he is a tool Shaun uses to make excuses for his life. Ed is literally the chain the binds Shaun, but is ultimately the final implement for Shaun's salvation and rebirth.

Liz controls Shaun by making plans and giving him ultimatums when he fails to do as she wishes. His failure to act as an equal partner places Liz in the position of superiority in that she feels she is an adult and he is not ("Oh grow up Shaun!"). When she breaks up with him, he becomes obsessed with winning her back, not by changing his behaviors, but by a childlike temper tantrum, or "acting out" as a thwarted child might. When they are forced to work together to survive the zombie attacks, Shaun finally steps up to the plate and shows his maturity, allowing Liz to stand beside him as an equal partner.

When Shaun awakens from his drunken stupor, his own words are facing him, written in ink on a dry erase board (and therefore not permanent): "Go round mums, get Liz back, sort out life!" When he finally realizes that they are ensconced in a full out zombie apocalypse, Shaun steps up to the plate and leads a rag-tag band of survivors. He shifts from res *corporealis* to a state of res *cognitas* as he begins to think and formulate a plan of action. That he is able to convince the others to follow him is indicative of an always present, but previously unexplored, ability to effectively lead a group of people: to cut the metaphorical umbilical cords. The people in the group he leads are all killed, except for himself and Liz. Through the blood and pain of losing each friend and family member one by one, he is ushered from a state of perpetual codependency to independent behavior.

When Zombies bite Ed, Shaun's best friend, Ed performs what is probably the only selfless act of his entire life: he stays behind to give Shaun and Liz a chance to escape. Shaun has reached Eudaimonia through Ed by Ed's act of staying behind when the zombies are breaking through the cellar door and by being the one who uses the lift to save Shaun and Liz. Liz is literally born with Shaun in this process. Together they survive the onslaught at the Winchester Pub, but are delivered by Ed to safety. Shaun and Liz's maturity was due to Ed becoming the vessel. Shaun's birthing experience begins in the film's climax, when he is forced to kill his biological mother, Barbara after she is bitten by a zombie. The pain and anguish is evident when he severs his life-long umbilical cord from Barbara and is left in the cellar with the newly bitten Ed and his girlfriend Liz. Ed, knowing that his life is over and feeling the zombie virus coursing through him, delivers Shaun and Liz to their new lives as he pushes the button to the lift and the bright light of the new world births Shaun and Liz from the dark, womb-like cellar. The imagery is that of childbirth, life and hope…the very nature of pregnancy and Shaun's new life was brought to us by Ed, former lay-about turned zombie, who subsequently is leading a life he ultimately desired as well…no responsibilities and playing video games with his best mate (undeath in a Zombie Shed out back). This is Ed's personal Eudaimonia.

This paper analyzes how through the experience of zombie apocalypse, the characters of Helen Robinson and Shaun are metaphorically "birthed" into a new shiny life in which they find Eudaimonia: a state of true happiness that was lacking in their previous lives prior to zombie introductions. Both Shaun and Helen are rewarded with love, friends, family and wealth upon their survival of the birthing process of blood, pain and loneliness as well as stagnation of their life pre-zombie. Their new "Zombie Mums" are ultimately kept in their lives as enrichment and not the ties that bound them so as with their previous existence. Although Fido is both lover and Mother to Helen, he remains in her life as a partner. Ed remains with Shaun in his shed, a fun friend to hang with on weekends to play video games with, but no longer holding Shaun back, but complementing his now hopeful life. The prospect of life through an undead parent is presented through the blood, pain, and labors that Helen and Shaun experience…in essence, their own births. Their lives are given to them by zombie mums.

Works Cited

Cole, Phillip. "Rousseau and the Vampires: Towards a Political Philosophy of the Undead." The Undead and Philosophy. Ed. Richard Greene and K. Silem Mohammad. Peru, IL: Open Court, 2006. 169-182.

Fido. Dir. Andrew Currie. Perf. Carrie-Anne Moss, Billy Connelly. 2007. DVD. Lionsgate Films, 2006.

Jacquette, Dale. "Zombie Gladiators." The Undead and Philosophy. Ed. Richard Greene and K. Silem Mohammad. Peru, IL: Open Court, 2006. 105-118.

Larkin, William S. "Res Corporealis: Persons, Bodies and Zombies." The Undead and Philosophy. Ed. Richard Greene and K. Silem Mohammad. Peru, IL: Open Court, 2006. 15-26.

Shaun of the Dead. Dir. Edgar Wright. Perf. Simon Pegg, Kate Ashfield, Nick Frost. 2004. DVD. Studio Canal, 2004.

Thompson, Hamish. "'She's Not Your Mother Anymore, She's a Zombie!': Zombies, Value, and Personal Identity." The Undead and Philosophy. Ed. Richard Greene and K. Silem Mohammad. Peru, IL: Open Court, 2006. 27-38.

Walker, Matthew. "When There's No More Room in Hell, the Dead Will Shop the Earth: Romero and Aristotle on Zombies, Happiness and Consumption." The Undead and Philosophy. Ed. Richard Greene and K. Silem Mohammad. Peru, IL: Open Court, 2006. 81-90.

APPENDIX

The Legend by Steve Cook - 1987

A cool summer morning in early June, is when the legend began, at a nameless loggin' camp in Wexford County, where the Manistee River ran. Eleven lumberjacks near the Garland swamp found an animal they thought was a dog. In a playful mood they chased it around till it ran inside a hollow log. A logger named Johnson grabbed him a stick and poked around inside. Then the thing let out an unearthly scream and came out and stood upright.

None of those men ever said very much, 'bout what ever happened then. They just packed up their belongings and left that night, were never heard from again.

It was ten years later in '97, when a farmer near Buckley was found. Slumped over his plow, his heart had stopped, there were dog tracks all around.

Seven years passed with the turn of the century, they say a crazy old wida' had a dream, of dogs that circled her house at night that walked like men and screamed.

In 1917, a sheriff who was out walkin found a driverless wagon and tracks in the dust, like wolves had been a stalkin'. Near the roadside a four-horse team lay dead with their eyes open wide. When the vet finished up his examination, he said it looked like they died of fright.

In '37 a schooner captain said, several crew members had reported a pack of wild dogs roaming Bowers Harbor. His story was never recorded.

In '57 a man of the cloth found claw marks on an old church door. The newspaper said they'd been made by a dog, he'd a had to stood 7'4."

In '67 a van-load of hippies, told a park-ranger named Quinlinn, they'd been awakened in the night by a scratch at the winda'… there was a dogman looking in and grinnin'.

In '77 there were screams in the night, near the village of Bellaire. Could've been a bobcat, could've been the wind, nobody looked up there.

Then in the summer of '87, near Luther, it happened again…at a cabin in the woods it looked like maybe, someone had tried to break in. There were cuts around the doors that could only been made by very sharp teeth and claws. He didn't wear shoes cuz he didn't have feet. He walked on just two paws.

In 1997, final part of the song was updated to include this lyric:

So far this year, no stories have appeared. Have the dogmen gone away? Have they disappeared? Soon enough I guess we'll know, cuz this is the time to fear, cuz in this decade called the 80's, the seventh year is here… and somewhere in the north-woods darkness, a creature walks upright. And the best advice you may ever get is never to go out….at night.

Turn the page for an exclusive

special preview of

FINDING STELLA:
THE UNLIKELY ADVENTURE OF A SILICONE WEREWOLF AND I

a new book by author

Sally L. Gage

Excerpt from *FINDING STELLA*
PREFACE

Most folks at one point or another in their lives find themselves saying "These are difficult times"… Whether it be in a time of war, famine, family disagreement, or deciding which pair of socks to wear the sentiment is the same: you are being faced with a decision to move forward facing an unknown. Sometimes people are so bogged down in situations that they have already survived that facing a fork in the road of the unknowing turns their brain around and they live the rest of their lives facing backwards, trying to analyze the future from their past events but all they see is their own ass. They get "Spun."

People who have perhaps suffered a tragedy or the opposite (have had great elation) are sometimes perpetually stuck in a loop of confusion waiting for their lives to happen or anything to happen, only having the monotony of existence punctuated by random good and bad events that the brain denies as fleeting, never fully enjoying or feeling the moment when it is upon them. Forever they are striving to escape or recapture that pivotal moment that caused the spin to start and never achieving it; just spinning in a circle chasing their tails in a perpetual loop that blinds them to the outside world. All the while, they are wondering "Does this get better?" or "One of these days I'm gonna…" Just like me.

I was in this spin when I was facing the greatest precipice of my life while I was researching a paper about werewolves. Lazily clicking through page after page of pictures in my search for the perfect piece to grace the cover of my essay I saw them. WerePups.

An artist named Asia Eriksen had begun making little latex werewolves that were reminiscent of the childhood dolls I used to play with but with a puppy type face that was just too cute for words. I bookmarked the page and bean to follow her work and very shortly after words she began making life sized silicone baby werewolves. The very first picture I saw was an adorable picture of Asia holding Ezra, it looked so lifelike and so adorable that my little heart just melted, and I proclaimed, "I WILL OWN ONE OF THESE!" I then contacted Asia and began the adoption process of getting my very own baby werewolf, whom I planned from the start to call "Stella."

So, I had entered the realm of reborn dolls. A creepy place where folks with amazing artistic skills reimagine childhood favorites into lifelike pieces of art. I had seen some over the years but had never "gotten into" them, as I have a kind of a love/hate relationship with human dolls. "Alternative reborns" are a branch from the regular human baby dolls in that these dolls are turn into monsters or aliens or werewolves. Sometimes grotesque, sometimes adorable but always artistically delivered and displayed. Such is the case with WerePups.

Once the down payment and description of my doll was delivered to Asia, I announced my impending pup purchase on social media, where I learned a new phrase…I was "Reborn Pregnant." I was embraced and celebrated like an expectant mother would have been in real life. I admit I was a little weirded out at first, but hey folks were saying nice things and celebrating my new doll with such joy, so who am I to judge?

This was the spring of 2012 and my life was about to turn completely around.

Remember how I spoke about being spun? Well at this time I had no job and we were struggling, but I did little odds jobs to drop the down payment for my pup. Around this time, my Father had also just told me that he was sick and even though he had previously told me he was fine, I knew the diagnosis of Mesothelioma was 100% fatal, so it was just a matter of time. Finally, just as I was adjusting to everything else, funding for my graduate courses was cut off and I could no longer go to school; literally three classes and one master's thesis away from graduation.

I fell into the abyss. Despair, humiliation, and grief triggered my ever-present anxieties into high gear and were kind enough to give me new ones as well, like panic attacks from florescent lights or if someone looked at me I would burst into tears and hide. Not very fun for a (then) 45-year-old lady.

By the time 2013 chimed into life, my darling wife Leisa had us settled into a more frugal routine and we were existing, but we couldn't afford the fineries in life. I could make payments on my WerePup and all was starting to look brighter, as I had found a job at the History museum which, although only part time, kept our heads above water and gave me a sense of dignity I so desperately needed.

By April though, my father's health had declined, and I knew the end was near. On April 29th, I received the phone call I was dreading: Richard Gage, my father, my rock, my Obi-wan, had walked on that morning to the great unknown. Nothing was left unsaid between us, my father and I, no regrets no animosity, nothing but love and honesty. I will cherish our philosophical conversations and our silly chatter. No one has a perfect childhood, but I think I came pretty darned close.

I immediately notified work and Leisa and I left for Manistee, Michigan within the hour.

After returning to Florida from Michigan. life settled back down to normal home/work life, but I found I could no longer go into a grocery store or a pharmacy without a massive panic attack. If crowds got too big in the museum, I would shake and sweat like a sinner in church. If people touched me, I would jerk away like I had been burned by their touch. I was sad and miserable, and inevitably my father would wander through my thoughts and the tears would flow.

Like many who suffer from anxiety, I was prescribed a nice sedative to take the edge off because amidst all this, I was planning my wedding. My honeymoon was set to be at Dragon*Con (small intimate gathering of about 87,000 nerds) in Atlanta, Georgia and my anxiety was off the chart. The cost was going to be high. The bills for the wedding started to rear their ugly little heads and the collective cost of everything transferring from single to married life was mounting…

Then on August 25th, two days before we left for Dragon*Con, Stella, my WerePup, came home.

COMING SOON FROM LEISA A. CLARK

COMING SOON FROM SALLY L. GAGE

FINDING STELLA IS A TRUE STORY OF HOW A SILICONE DOLL CAME INTO
THE LIFE OF A COLLEGE STUDENT ON THE BRINK OF LOSING HER
FUNDING FOR SCHOOL, LOSING HER JOB AND LOSING HER FATHER AND
HOW THIS LITTLE WEREWOLF NAMED STELLA SENT HER LIFE IN
DIRECTIONS SHE ONLY EVER DREAMED OF. JOIN SALLY AS SHE TELLS
YOU HOW WAS SAVED BY FINDING STELLA.

MOLLIE AND TASHA SHEPHERD DO NOT WANT MUCH OUT OF LIFE. A ROOF OVER THEIR HEADS, FOOD TO EAT, ROCK AND ROLL, AND THE PERFECT SHADE OF NAIL POLISH…WHAT THEY WIND UP WITH IS THE ADVENTURE OF A LIFETIME. RECRUITED AFTER ANSWERING A HIGHLY SUSPICIOUS PERSONAL AD (I KNOW, RIGHT?). IN THE COMPANY OF TWO MUSICAL SCOTSMEN, A TALKING DOG, A REBEL FLEEING FROM THE VINYL RECORD POLICE, THE ULTIMATE FABULOUS HAIRDRESSER, AND THE SLEAZIEST OF SLEAZY BAND MANAGERS, THEY STEAL A SPACESHIP AND SHATTER THE PARAMETERS OF SPACE, TIME, AND PLAUSIBLE STORYLINES IN A SATIRICAL/PARODY SCI-FI ADVENTURE STEEPED IN 90'S POP CULTURE AND OUTRAGEOUS HIJINKS THAT HAVE TO BE SEEN TO BE BELIEVED. NO, REALLY, YOU HAVE TO SEE THEM. JUST BUY THE BOOK!

FIRST EDITION 2017   ISBN-10: 1976357160 / ISBN-13: 978-1976357169
COVER DEISGN BY RUTH KEYES / COVER ART BY GENEVRA BROWN

IN THIS SERIES OF POP CULTURE ESSAYS, AUTHOR AND EDITOR LEISA A. CLARK TAKES A TRIP DOWN MEMORY LANE TO WHERE HER WORK ON POP CULTURE NARRATIVES BEGAN: AS A GRADUATE STUDENT. WITH ESSAYS ON XENA: WARRIOR PRINCESS, BUFFY THE VAMPIRE SLAYER, BABYLON 5, HORROR MUSICALS, YA POST-APOCALYPSE NOVELS, AND HARRY POTTER, THIS BOOK EXPLORES THEMES SUCH AS LOVE, IDENTITY, AND HORROR, AND SERVES TO ILLUSTRATE HER DIVERSITY OF INTEREST WHILE PROVIDING KEEN INSIGHT INTO MULTIPLE MASS MEDIA.

FIRST PRINT AUGUST 2018
COVER DESIGN BY SALLY GAGE / MYSTICAL HODGEPODGE
ISBN-13: 978-1723479939 / ISBN-10: 1723479934

N 1990S TAMPA, A YOUNG WOMAN BORED WITH LIFE AND EAGER TO EXPLORE HER BOUNDARIES IS DRAWN INTO A WORLD OF MYSTERY, MURDER, PASSION, AND INTRIGUE...AND LOVE. JOHANNA IS YOUNG WOMAN WHO DESIRES IMMORTALITY. MARYN IS AN IMMORTAL WHO OFFERS PLEASURE AND PAIN. TOGETHER, THEY WILL TAKE A JOURNEY THAT WILL CHANGE THEM FOREVER.

THE PHANTOMS COLLECTION
BY SADIE BLACKBURN

A COLLECTION OF GHOST STORIES FEATURING BRAVE FEMALE
PROTAGONISTS WHO FACE THEIR OWN FEARS TO RIGHT LONG AGO
WRONGS FOR THE SAKE OF PHANTOMS WHO COME TO THEM FOR HELP.

NEW FROM SADIE BLACKBURN

THE MANSION OF THE FAMOUS LATE AUTHOR GEORGE LYNDON
ADDISON HAS BEEN DONATED TO THE STATE OF NEW YORK WITH THE
INTENTION OF TURNING IT INTO A MUSEUM. IN THE MONTHS BEFORE
THE MUSEUM IS TO OPEN, SAM FORRESTER, HISTORIAN AND BIOGRAPHER,
IS HIRED TO SPEND A SUMMER ON THE PROPERTY, RESEARCHING
MATERIAL FOR HIS UPCOMING ADDISON BIOGRAPHY. IN THE WAKE OF A
DIVORCE, HE BRINGS HIS DAUGHTER ADDIE WITH HIM TO SPEND THE
SUMMER IN THE MANSION. IT DOES NOT TAKE LONG BEFORE
MYSTERIOUS HAPPENINGS BEGIN TO SUGGEST THAT BOTH ADDIE AND
THE MANSION ITSELF ARE BEING HAUNTED BY A MYSTERIOUS CHILD IN
ANTIQUE CLOTHING, WHO WALKS THE SHADOWY HALLS BY NIGHT AND
WHISPERS AT WINDOWSILLS. WHAT THE LONELY SPIRIT WANTS AND HOW
ADDIE CAN HELP HER IS NOT AT FIRST CLEAR, BUT BEFORE THE STORY IS
OVER, THE LOST LITTLE GHOST WILL EITHER SAVE THE YOUNG GIRL'S
LIFE—OR TAKE IT FOR HER OWN.

THE PENTECOST CHRONICLES
BY SADIE BLACKBURN

AS THE OLD SAYING GOES, SOME ARE BORN GREAT, SOME ACHIEVE GREATNESS, SOME HAVE GREATNESS THRUST UPON THEM. THEN AGAIN, SOME MEET GREATNESS FOR A COUPLE OF BEERS ON A FRIDAY NIGHT, AND NEVER SEND IT PACKING. THE PENTECOST CHRONICLES, BY SADIE BLACKBURN. AN ALTERNATE VICTORIAN ADVENTURE SERIES FILLED WITH SWASHBUCKLING HEROES, DARING, DANGER AND STEAMPUNK DIRIGIBLES. THE ADVENTURE WILL FIND YOU ANYWAY, YOU MIGHT AS WELL GO OUT AND MEET IT.

COMING SOON FROM SADIE BLACKBURN

REVENGE IS NOT ALWAYS BEST SERVED COLD—AND IT IS NOT ALWAYS A SOLITARY ENDEAVOR. SOMETIMES REVENGE FINDS A PURPOSE, A PROMISE…AND A PARTNER. DESMOND GRIFFIN, FORTY-NINE YEARS AND SIX FOOT THREE OF RAKISH PIRATE IN A VELVET GREAT COAT, IS DRIVEN BY IT. STRONG AS STEEL, SEEKING TO AVENGE THE MURDER OF HIS SON, AND UNAFRAID TO CHALLENGE THE DEVIL TO DO IT. HE HAS JUSTICE TO SERVE AND A DEBT TO BE PAID AND WILL BROOK NO COMPLICATIONS. ARRINGTON PENTECOST IS PRECISELY SUCH A COMPLICATION. OF ALL THE STUDENTS WHO MIGHT HAVE STUMBLED UPON HIS RESPECTED PROFESSOR'S SECRET IDENTITY, PENTECOST MIGHT HAVE BEEN VOTED MOST LIKELY TO BE DISASTROUS. TRACKING HIS SUSPICIONS THROUGH THE DEAD OF THE NIGHT, PENTECOST DISCOVERS THAT THE MEN HE THOUGHT WERE VILLAINS ARE ACTUALLY VIGILANTES, AND THAT THE ONLY THING STANDING BETWEEN INNOCENT VICTIMS AND THE REAL THREAT ARE A BAND OF BRAVE AND FOOLHARDY HEROES UNAFRAID TO RISK EVERYTHING. WHETHER THE TRUE VILLAINS, DANGEROUS AND DEADLY SHADOWS FROM HIS OWN PAST, CAN BE DEFEATED REMAINS TO BE SEEN, BUT PENTECOST IS CERTAIN OF TWO THINGS AS HE PLUNGES INTO INTRIGUE ON THE HEELS OF DESMOND GRIFFIN. REVENGE WILL ONLY WAIT SO LONG TO BE PAID—AND THE PRICE MIGHT BE MORE THAN ANY OF THEM HAD BARGAINED FOR

ABOUT THE AUTHOR

Sally Gage was born and raised in the little town of Manistee, Michigan. A mixed blood child of an Ojibwe father and Irish/German mother she was a wild child of the woods and could scarcely be found indoors let alone with clothes on. Her best friends were a cat named Jinx, a mangy dog named Perky, and rooster called Mr. Grinch. With them, she learned how to communicate with the animals around her better than the kids in the neighborhood. When she was in high school her love of animals and horror movies kicked in.

Sally now lives in Florida with her wife, a pack of WerePups, and clowder of cats. The full moon still looks over her life and the passion or werewolf movies still pumps her heart. This book is just the first, a toe in the ocean, of writing for yo-yos who love strange things. Maybe this simple literary work will encourage the next generation to follow their passion no matter how weird, wild or odd it may be. Chase your werewolf little one, run.

AaaaaaaaAAAArrrrroooooOOO000ooooo

www.ingramcontent.com/pod-product-compliance
Lightning Source LLC
Chambersburg PA
CBHW051311250726
48656CB00004B/1594